CHOOSING HAPPINESS

The decisions you choose, will determine
the life you'll have

RICO ITUARTE

BALBOA.
PRESS

A DIVISION OF HAY HOUSE

Balboa Press books may be ordered through booksellers or by contacting:

Balboa Press
A Division of Hay House
1663 Liberty Drive
Bloomington, IN 47403
www.balboapress.com
1 (877) 407-4847

Because of the dynamic nature of the Internet, any web addresses or
links contained in this book may have changed since publication and
may no longer be valid. The views expressed in this work are solely those
of the author and do not necessarily reflect the views of the publisher,
and the publisher hereby disclaims any responsibility for them.

The author of this book does not dispense medical advice or prescribe the use
of any technique as a form of treatment for physical, emotional, or medical
problems without the advice of a physician, either directly or indirectly. The
intent of the author is only to offer information of a general nature to help
you in your quest for emotional and spiritual well-being. In the event you use
any of the information in this book for yourself, which is your constitutional
right, the author and the publisher assume no responsibility for your actions.

Any people depicted in stock imagery provided by Thinkstock are
models, and such images are being used for illustrative purposes only.
Certain stock imagery © Thinkstock.

Print information available on the last page.

ISBN: 978-1-5043-6096-8 (sc)
ISBN: 978-1-5043-6095-1 (hc)
ISBN: 978-1-5043-6097-5 (e)

Library of Congress Control Number: 2016910486

Balboa Press rev. date: 02/03/2017

Contents

Chapter 1

Why Me?

Who am I to write this book?

What kind of authority can I say I have in order for you to believe what I am about to tell you?

> *"Happiness is not something you postpone for the future; it is something you design for the present."*
>
> *-Jim Rohn 1930-2009, author and speaker-*

You probably opened this book, because you were curious about how you could be happy or happier than you are now.

Don't just believe what I say. Instead, perform some of the recommended exercises in this book. If, just if, you become happier, *then* apply these principles on a daily basis. Experience the results for yourself.

Early in childhood, I realized that all human beings are looking for happiness, each in their own way. A great number of us believe that when we acquire a beautiful or bigger home, we will be happy. That when we get the car of our dreams, we'll be happy. That the day we find the perfect significant other, we will be happy. Or, when we finally have babies with them or have enough money then, surely then, we will be happy. So we are always postponing our expectation for happiness in the belief that things or relationships will make us happy. Unfortunately, that day never arrives. Meanwhile, we waste our lives in search of the always evasive happiness. It never quite comes within our reach.

My background and experience on being happy is as universal as anyone's. It began in my early youth. I was born into Catholicism and my parents (who were devout) used to take me to Mass every Sunday.

For some reason, I used to faint in the middle of Mass and my father would have to take me out. Doctors never found what caused my fainting spells. They speculated I may have had a heart condition (I just turned sixty eight. I don't think it was heart condition). Some doctors said it may have been the air quality in the church due the amount of people and poor ventilation. That a lack of oxygen was the cause of my dilemma. I don't remember most of the reasons, my parents didn't tell me all of them, but it was a large enough concern for everyone to have an opinion on the matter.

My guess is that as a little boy, I was impressed with the figures and sculptures inside the church, especially with those of Jesus bathed in blood and the expression of suffering beyond the understanding of a child. The image of open wounds in his chest, the hands and feet penetrated by those big, rusted, and dirty nails full of blood coming out of his body. That vivid impression was what made me faint as a child. It was that simple.

I could not stand the pain and suffering, not from Jesus, nor from any creature. It didn't matter if it ranged from insects being smashed to owners hitting and punishing pets for what they perceived was bad behavior. So, from the beginning of my life, I noticed there was pain and pleasure. Through my Catholic upbringing, I learned about Paradise. It was the place where

God had put Adam and Eve **to be eternally happy and joyful.** So, from a young age, I questioned myself, **Why are we not happy and joyful? What happened to the Paradise we were born into?** (There are different opinions on the meaning of the words *happy and joy*, see the definitions and make your own analysis and meaning of the words, in the website below).

http://www.diffen.com/difference/Happiness_vs_Joy

> *"We all long for heaven where God is, but we have it in our power*
> *to be in heaven with him right now--to be happy with him at this*
> *very moment. But being happy with Him now means:*
> *loving as He loves,*
> *helping as He helps,*
> *giving as He gives,*
> *serving as He serves,*
> *rescuing as He rescues,*
> *being with Him for all the twenty-four hours,*
> *touching Him in His distressing disguise."*
>
> *-MOTHER TERESA-*

I was a teen when the citizen band (CB) radio became popular. I purchased one and as many of you might know, we had nicknames to identify ourselves on the air. Well, for some reason, my subconscious mind at the age of sixteen suddenly said to me, **"Your CB radio handle is: Happy.** "It was as if something inside me was telling me that I either wanted, desired, was able to, had to be, or had already inside of me; **THE ABILITY TO BE HAPPY!**

In my early twenties, I made a trip I to the south of Mexico. Cancun was in the beginning stages of its development. I was with friends and my daughter was only two years old at the time. We were using CB radios to communicate between three cars and I again used my old CB handle, "Happy". The trip was great and I remember being at the center of happiness and joy for everyone on the trip. My daughter's name is **Azulinda** and in Spanish, gasoline, is spelled **"gasolina"**. The ending sounds of my daughter's name Azulinda and gasolina are very similar. She wanted to use the radio and communicated with my friends. When they asked what her handle was, we came up with, **"Gasolina"**. The whole group had a great time and we all laughed during the trip.

> *"We tend to forget that happiness doesn't come as a result of getting something we don't have, but rather of recognizing and appreciating what we do have."*
>
> -Frederick Keonig-

So what qualifies me to write about happiness? Well, from my childhood, I started practicing being happy for no apparent reason. I've read books, gone to seminars, studied NLP (Neuro-Linguistic Programming, a science of the subconscious mind), and have practiced what I've learned. Due to the practice of the following principles described in this book, I've been able to create happiness on a moment by moment basis and even during the most difficult periods of my life.

During my sixty eight years of life, I've practiced what I've learned from a wide variety of authors. I've put into practice what they say about happiness and living in the **NOW**. Eckhart Tolle teaches this principle in his book, "The Power of Now."

A personal example of engaging in the practice of being happy without paying attention to any of my circumstances was this: following two ankle surgeries (one in June 2011 and the other one in February 2013) I had been in continuous pain for over two and a half years. While I was writing this in August of 2013, I was waking up every morning with searing pain in my right ankle. On the pain scale of zero to ten, I had a level eight.

Now, did I let the pain ruin my days, my nights or any moment in which I can decide my happiness? Not at all. I practice what I teach; nothing can make me unhappy. Wouldn't you like to know why? Because I *choose happiness* over anything else. *Happiness is a choice.*

Below are photos of two of the surgeries I had in June 2011 and February 2013. Maybe they can do a better job in illustrating the pain I have had for over two years. Yet, even this pain has not taken away my *choice* for daily happiness. In this first photo, you can see seven metal rods, --three on the back of my foot and two in each ring around my leg-- a total of seven metal rods crossing my leg from side to side and through the bones. The surgeons had to drill through the bones to put the rods in.

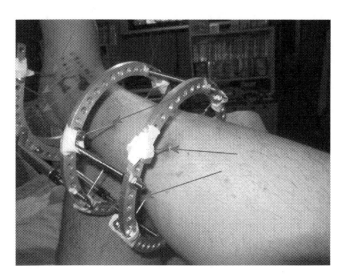

This next photo shows you the results of the second surgery. Here, I only had three rods crossing through the bones. However, even though there were only three, they were bigger, wider, and more painful. The red arrows in the picture point at the three bigger rods.

* Update: In August 2014, I had my fourth surgery. My ankle was replaced, and finally the pain is almost gone.

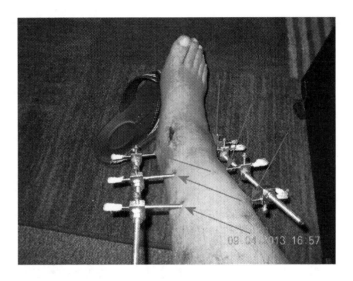

The surgery was needed due to a destruction and loss of cartilage located in the gaps where the leg and feet bones connect. Every step I took was incredibly painful because of the bones rubbing against each other. The loss of cartilage originally began after a fracture in 1998 following a motorcycle accident where I was attempting to ride a huge hill (after not having being on a motorcycle for many years). I was climbing it on a cross-country model and fell down in the middle of the attempt. The initial fall did nothing to me. However, when I tried to lift and turn the bike, my left foot slipped on the dirt and the bike fell on my right ankle. The weight of it broke the tibia and fibula bones. When the doctors performed surgery on my leg and put the bones back together, it took seven screws and a metal plate to hold the bones back. They (the doctors) warned me I could eventually develop arthrosis on the joint and it could destroy the cartilage. Well guess what? They were planting that seed into my subconscious mind, and I wound up creating that particular condition.

Even so, despite the constant physical pain, I chose happiness. This is an example of what I practice regarding the happiness choice. However, there are other types of pain, like emotional pain. Maybe you believe that emotional pain is harder to overcome.

You might not believe emotional pain can be removed by choice and that is fine. I agree with you. There are very difficult moments in life that can take happiness away from anyone.

When people tell me that there will be situations in which I will not be able to choose happiness, I usually tell them my personal story. It relates to individuals, who have either gone through or will go through difficulties of losing a loved one. To most, those moments appear to be insurmountable and filled with pain. In contrast and with time, most of us can dilute the pain.

I mean moments like when a loved one had passed on. In this case I will talk about when my mother (who I loved dearly) passed away. She died in my arms. I have to recognize that in that exact moment I experienced a pain that is not physical, but profound in the heart of the soul. After a few minutes passed, I called my siblings and told them what just happened. Our mother had passed. Each of our reactions was different. We chose to feel differently from each other and while it was the same event, there were three distinct reactions to this event. The "event" was that my mother died.

My perception of my sister's feelings, was something like this: "It was better for her. It was her time." And then she cried. My younger brother didn't want to come to the hospital and I still don't know his feelings. He was probably upset and because he didn't show up, I have no idea of what his reaction was or the kind of pain he was suffering. I know that he was likely who felt more attached to her.

Following my sister's arrival to the hospital where my mother died, the doctor came into the room and asked us who would take care of the funeral. Since I was the oldest, I volunteered. I immediately left the room and started making calls to funeral homes and negotiate prices for services and casket. I had to take care of the funeral arrangements. I went out of my pain and took care of the details and all legal arrangements needed. I gave orders and faced the issues head on. It also included contacting the newspaper, family members, and looking for the things that needed to be taken care of. I was busy in giving orders and making constant decisions. In a moment of pause while I was on the telephone, I realized I was not feeling any kind of pain. None physically and none in my soul.

I realized that when I was **present**, and in the moment, I didn't feel pain. I was dealing with what the **now** needed. My attention was entirely focused on the negotiation of a funeral. I realized that as soon as I went into the past and remembered the moment of my mother dying, the pain came back, and don't get me wrong, I went back to that moment several times in the future months...crying in the middle of showering, at moments where nobody could see. I realize now, that the pain was present when I was thinking in the past. As soon as I had a problem to deal with; the pain disappeared and I was in the moment, the **now** again.

Pain and suffering can only exist in the past or future, but never in the present. Any pain occurring in the **now** flows into the past immediately. Within the next second, it's already in the past. I remembered having read a book from Eckhart Tolle, The Power of Now, and in that moment it clicked. Eckhart Tolle is right; by me dealing with the business of the funeral, I was living in the **now** and had no pain. As soon as I finished the negotiations and went back to the room where my mother was lying, I brought back the moment of her death. As soon as I did that, the pain came back. She had died just a few minutes ago. However, I had relinquished my pain by being in the now during my negotiations with the funeral home. I had studied Neuro-linguistic Programming previously and remembered a statement in NLP that says: "For the Subconscious Mind to actually 'experience' an event or to 'think 'about an event that has already happened is exactly the same". "To think or to do, is the same for the subconscious mind."

So, I decided to change my perspective regarding my mother's passing. I chose to see the positive side of the event and *reframed* the situation; I chose to be happy.

I was happy. I was happy for her. She no longer had to suffer and that made me happy. As you can see, the same event can bring different feelings and emotions. It is always about how I choose to feel after any event in my life. Do I mean to say it was easy to feel happy? Well, not at the beginning. Even so, I progressed from sadness to happiness in a short period and with time and practice, the sadness was reduced further and further.

I believed we could choose to feel happy at any moment. When that belief was tested at my mother's passing, it became the perfect opportunity to prove my thinking and I did. I felt happy even though my mother died. I thought of *all* the *positive* outcomes resulting from her death. For example, I realized she no longer suffered. I realized she will not have to live with the possibility of never speaking again (the doctor had removed her vocal cords in surgery) because she always spoke the truth and she would no longer be able to speak. So, I continued searching for every imaginable positive outcome resulting from her death. I was then able to transform my pain into happiness, not only for me, but also for her.

The issue at hand, is that most people don't live in the *now*. They live in the past or future. They worry about what could happen and it doesn't seem to let them be happy. They grieve or are upset about things in the past (which they can't change) and keep dwelling on those awful events. This does not allow them to be happy *now*. How do you want to live? Happy or unhappy? Being worried for a future that hasn't happened? Or remembering and re-living bad moments from your past with regrets or things someone did to you. All these things, *cannot be changed by you.*

There are things from your past that likely marked you for life. The mark is created by your *ego*. It is unable to forgive. It is the *ego* that always blames other people for what happened. If I was truly a victim in a particular event, the only way to remove that pain from the past is *to forgive*. Forgiveness is not for the other person involved in the event. Forgiveness works because it frees your mind and your subconscious to help you stop re-living the event. So, don't forgive the person or persons who wronged you for their sake. Forgive them for your own sake. If those people are no longer alive, you can write them letter expressing you forgive them and they no longer hold a weight on you. Then, when you finish forgiving them in writing, put that letter in an envelope and burn it. Send the smoke to those involved in the forgiveness. Remember, you are not doing the act of forgiveness for them, you are doing it for your own benefit.

There are those who have told me the cause of their suffering is because of someone's actions against them. One friend said she was really upset because her significant other had cheated on her with a younger woman. My friend was unhappy and suffering for years by remembering what he did to her. However, I asked her one day, if she knew how he was doing? She replied, "He is very happy with that woman. As a matter of fact, he is traveling to Europe right now with her and enjoying life."

I told her, "Can't you see? He is happy, because he forgot about you and is living the present. You on the other hand, you are living and re-living the past, suffering and unhappy. He doesn't even know you're suffering."And I asked her, "Does it make sense for you to live in the past and suffer? Do as he does, live the present, forgive him. Your being upset and angry at him, does not affect him at all, it only affects you. *Stop* being angry and forgive him. Start living in the present".

It is called *present* because is a gift of life, and you are not accepting your gift. You are living in the past, suffering by choice. I asked her, "Do you really think that by being unhappy, he will suffer?" She answered "no" to my question. She knew he was happy and her suffering would not affect him at all. From that day on, she decided to forgive him and started living in the *now*.

The formula to be happy then, is to make a conscious decision to be happy *now*. To enjoy each moment life in the present. It is the only moment we have. We do not have a tomorrow, neither a yesterday. If you live thinking about the things that happened and feeling sorry for them, you are re-living the same events. As I mentioned before, according to new discoveries of science and in Neuro-linguistic Programming for the Subconscious Mind, to think in any event is the same as to live the event. Your subconscious mind is then re-living those bad memories every time you bring them to your consciousness. That particular moment happened one time. However, you're living it as often as you remember. My suggestion is to live each moment with joy and intensity. Of being grateful for whatever your health status is *now*. That your: energy, smile, sight, limbs, heart, stomach, hair or lack of it (like me, I am almost bald) and enjoy that you can sweat because of the heat of the day. Or that you can enjoy the feel of cold because of the rain. That you can enjoy eating something even if it is only celery. To enjoy and be grateful that you can breathe. Do you know how many people stopped breathing today?

In each moment of our lives, we have the *option* to decide, *how we want to feel.* How do you want to feel today, in this moment? *It is your option and your decision.* You might say to yourself, "To decide to be happy is hard"!So to your statement that it is hard, let me share this quote from Neuro-linguistic Programming, "*It is as easy or as hard as you want to make it.*"

Deciding to be happy is as easy as standing up from a chair or lifting your arm. Can you raise your arm? If you can do that, then *you can also choose to be happy.* You can constantly and consciously choose to be *happy now.* It is your decision. Be happy every moment of your life.

You brush your teeth every day, don't you? Well, you can also create the habit of being happy as you created the habit of brushing your teeth. If you do it consistently and repeatedly, the habit of being happy will be created and you will be happy automatically. At the beginning it will be a conscious effort, but soon, it will be easier and easier to become happy for most of the day.

The only way to *be happy*, is to make a conscious decision to *be happy now*, in this precise moment. There are many scientific studies that claim that time, per say, does not exist, it is an illusion.

> *"There Is No Way to Happiness,*
> *Happiness Is the Way."*
>
> -*Thich Nhat Hanh*-

Consider this practical exercise that demonstrates the nonsense of the concept of time. Think about the East coast of the US, Florida or Washington, D.C. Let's say an event is happening there at 11:00 in the morning. The event is so important, that people on the West coast are so interested in the event that it will be televised. The broadcast will be at 11:00 AM Eastern time. So, at what time will people in California have to watch the broadcast? With the three hour difference, they will be watching at 8:00 AM. However, the event is happening at the same moment in both places. The event is not happening at two different times in two different places, it is one event at one time in two differently labeled times created by society.

If you could travel by rocket to the International Space Station, you would see that particular event from space as it occurred. You would also see both parties on the west and east coasts watching the same event at the same time.

Furthermore, let me ask you a question (think carefully before you answer). Can you do something in this precise moment that will change your yesterday? Or, can you do something in this precise moment like it is tomorrow? No! You can't! You can only do things *now*! There is only *now*! No past, no future, they do not exist in the *now*. *Past* and *future* are only concepts that do not exist. You can't do anything before or after. You can only do or live *now*. You can't change what you did in the past, and you can't do now what you are going to be doing some day in the future. Why? Because when you do that, it will not be in the future, it will be in the *now*.

> "Happiness cannot be travel to, owned, earned, worn or consumed.
> Happiness is the spiritual
> experience of living
> every minute with love,
> grace and gratitude."
>
> -Denis Waitley-

Therefore, if you can't do anything in the past or the future, and you can only do things *now*, today, in this moment, I ask you: Can you make the decision to be happy *now*?

I invite you to start living in the *now* and know that it is possible to achieve living in the *now*. Then, when you master living in the now, you will feel joy and happiness all of the time. This concept *is a choice*. Choose to be in the present and when you do, you are choosing to be happy.

**"The decisions you choose, will
determine the life you'll have"**

Choose wisely.

C h a p t e r 2

HDAV Cause-Effect

I began wondering and asking myself, "What is something that everyone really wants?"

I came to a conclusion and dared to say everyone wants to be happy. There maybe a few who don't want to be happy because their suffering, brings them happiness. Or maybe those few have been programmed to not believe in the possibility of happiness. What they do not realize yet, is that a person can change their program if they choose to.

I believe we all want to be happy, and a way to get that happiness is finally here.

This book is about choices. You've read in the previous chapter:

> **"The decisions you choose, will**
> **determine the life you'll have"**

Everything in this life is a choice.

At every moment, each of us have the opportunity to choose. We can choose to either stay in bed or get out of bed and do something. We can choose to take a shower or not. We can choose what clothing to wear. We can choose to have breakfast or go out on an empty stomach. We can choose whether to work or not. We are choosing all throughout the day, all of the time. We make choices between fear and love. Our most important daily choices determine our state of mind. Happiness depends on whether we choose to live in the present, past or future.

> *"Each morning when I open my eyes*
> *I say to myself: I, not events,*
> *have the power to make me happy*
> *or unhappy today.*
> *I can choose which it shall be. Yesterday is dead, tomorrow*
> *hasn't arrived yet.*
> *I have just one day, today,*
> *and I'm going to be*
> *happy in it."*
>
> *-Groucho Marx-*

For those of you who know about the theory of Memes, you know that once you made the choice to read to the end this book, the *"virus of the mind"* that is within this book, will be on your mind forever. You will be *happy by choice*.

If you want to know about Memes, you can read about this very interesting subject in the book, Virus of the Mind, The New Science of the Meme by Richard Brodie. (Richard Brodie was Microsoft chairman and Bill Gates' personal technical assistant and the original author of Microsoft Word, one of the world's best-selling computer programs. Educated at Harvard, he is also the best-selling author of Getting Past OK.)

What if I tell you that what you and everyone else wants is a virus, a "meme" in the mind. A very powerful meme. To which you would probably say, "What? A meme virus? No, I don't think so. I don't want to be infected with any meme or virus". What if the meme I am talking about is one that is actually *good for you* and it is something you would like to have, because it would make you *happy*, very *happy all the time.*?

WARNING!

HDAV. A very powerful meme. A meme of the mind inoculating anybody that comes in contact with it. If you choose to keep reading, you will have the HDAV meme in your mind. You can stop here or keep reading. The HDAV Meme stands for:

Happy
Days
Always
Virus

You've been WARNED!
Will you dare to keep reading this book?
It is *your* choice and I know you want to be *happy*.

> *"I caught the happiness virus last night. When I was out singing beneath the stars."*
>
> *-Hafiz of Persia-*

Pain and Suffering Choices

Some people often ask, "Why do human beings experience pain and suffering?" When I heard this question I thought, "What pain and suffering is for one person, is not equal to another person's concept of pain and suffering". We all have different concepts and ideas. All of those ideas are based on our *personal experience*. You are (right there where you are sitting reading this book) the total sum of your experiences during the time span of your life. Your concept of pain and suffering is based solely on your personal experiences of what those are. You act, think and behave the way you do because of the programs that formed your personality and because of the personal knowledge you have accumulated. If you had lived in a different country and experienced a different culture, you would be thinking and behaving in a different way.

What is suffering for you, might well be a pleasure for someone else who had different experiences. For example, some people enjoy a ride on a rollercoaster to the fullest. While others may suffer tremendously just from the idea of riding that same rollercoaster. Do you understand that what you choose to call suffering, is just your personal perception of what suffering is? Therefore, perceiving or identifying pain and suffering, is also personal choice.

Another way of suffering as mentioned previously, is the fact that some people choose to not live in the *now*. Most people do not consciously realize that the past is gone and the future has yet to come. That the past and future are only illusions. Pain and suffering always come from experiences we have had. (Remember, we all are the sum of our experiences and the interpretations we have created from those experiences.)

We also suffer because of what we are expecting to endure in the future.

If I choose to accept the now as it is and to be grateful for what I am currently experiencing, I can then choose to see the present as *perfect* and nothing is wrong with this moment. This moment is just as *perfect* as it can be and I accept it for what it is.

If I can think and feel this way, I will automatically feel happy in the *now*.

There is a quote attributed to Benjamin Disraeli, 1804-1881, the British politician and author who was twice prime minister of Great Britain. Paraphrasing, the quote says something like this:

"Man lives crucified between two thieves; the regret of the Past and the worries of the future."

When we live like this (between regret and worry), we are rejecting and avoiding the happiness of the present. I suggest you live in the present where happiness resides and avoid past regrets or worrying about the future for things that may never happen.

> *"The secret of happiness*
> *is to admire without desiring."*
>
> *-Carl Sandburg-*

I recently listened to a guided meditation by Deepak Chopra in which he mentions the word "contentment." It brought to my attention that if we learn to be in contentment with what is happening at all times, we immediately eliminate the anxiety of fear, stress and worry.

So how easy is it for you to be in contentment with what is happening right now in your life? This is a big step towards choosing to be happy. Some of you will claim that it is very hard to be in contentment currently.

Consider repeating a formula I have practiced for years and which has made my life beautifully easy.

Here is my first gift to you: it is an affirmation that I personally repeat every day and very often. Practice saying this to yourself daily and as often as possible; the following affirmation works on anything you have to do or accomplish in your life. These words will change your life for the better and will make everything you do, be really easy to accomplish. Repeat the following statement every day as often as you can.

**"YES I CAN DO THIS. IT IS EASY AND
I AM GOING TO DO IT."**

I learned those words when I studied to become a practitioner of Neuro-linguistic programming. My teacher Fernando Arteche taught me this affirmation. I have been practicing and repeating the statement several times a day for over 20 years. Saying these words has made a big difference in my life. Since I started the practice of saying these words, everything I do is *EASY* and I know *I CAN DO IT!*

> *"Very little is needed to make a happy life; it is all within yourself, in your way of thinking"*
>
> *-Marcus Aurelius-*

How do you want to feel now and always? My guess is that you want to feel happy, secure, healthy and in a state of peace and *contentment*. I assure you that you can choose to feel the way you want to feel. I am convinced with certainty that you can feel the way you want just by choosing. I invite you to choose wisely.

The choice of pain and suffering versus the choice of happiness and joy is always our own, twenty four hours each of the seven days of the week.

Some will say there are present moments with pain and suffering because of an accident, a death in the family, a robbery or any other possible chaos that could be currently present, the *now* in our lives.

Reasonably, that is a valid observation. However, that particular moment is passing by. Also, and in a second more of time, it will already be in the past. If you then choose to keep lingering in the past and in remembrance of what just happened, there will be suffering and pain. How long do you want to keep remembering a loved one who has passed? How long do you want to suffer reliving the past and thinking about the loved one who has gone?

For many, the death of a loved one is a permanent event that is present for the rest of our lives. Even so, you can choose to remember that loved one in the best moments of their lives. How she or he was so full of love, life and happiness, and all the beautiful things they did for you and others. Or, you can choose to remember the precise moment of their death with all the suffering and pain. Can you choose to be happy remembering someone you love who is already gone? Yes you can! Just remember them in their best days and health.

In Chapter 1, I shared some of my personal history and when my mother died. That story will relate to moments in life every person will go through. To many, these moments appear to be insurmountable and very painful. As I learned when my mother died, the same event can bring different feelings and emotions. Because of our own experiences, each one of her children chose a different way to interpret the tragic event.

Every day of my life when I wake up, my first thought is: "How will I choose to feel after any event that could happen today in my life?" Do I mean it is easy to feel happy? Maybe not at the beginning. Slowly however, I have moved from sadness to happiness faster and faster. Some days I can do it right away and on others it takes more time. I now believe we can choose to feel happy at any moment and that each moment of my life happens to be the perfect moment because I choose it to be so.

How do you want to feel from now on? Decide, and choose for yourself. As I have said before, and will probably say it again, "choose wisely."

There are different types of choices. We can choose between two or more options. Some will say they would rather be silent or do nothing when confronted with a choice. However, not taking action is actually a choice. A choice of not making a choice. I have heard there are three types of people: the ones who make things happen (they take choices and risks); the ones who observe what others are doing and only join the group after they feel safe and secure and no further risk is involved (followers); and the ones who will eventually ask, "What happened?" Which type are you? Do you want to move to a different group? That is a choice, too.

What choices have you made until today? The choices you have made until now, have brought you to the place you are today. We begin making choices really young. When we are children, we learn that certain actions result in a response from our parents. So, we begin choosing to behave in a certain way to get what we want. Have you seen children throwing tantrums to get attention from their parents?

We make an unlimited amount of choices regarding everything from what we consume, wear, prepare for and so on. We also choose our friends and to accept or reject their ideas and behavior. In today's society, we hear how some young people make choices that ruin their lives by using drugs or engaging in unsafe sex. They end up as drug addicts living in the streets or with diseases that cut their lives short.

Always remember and commit to memory the following phrase: **"The decisions you choose, will determine the life you'll have"**

YOUR MOST IMPORTANT CHOICE
Cause or Effect: A Choice of Awareness
Do you choose to be the *cause* or do you choose to be the *effect?*

If you look at yourself in a mirror, you will see your reflected image. Now let me ask you something, is that reflection real? Some people will say that what they see in the mirror is real. However, if you move to one side, out of the range of the mirror, the image disappears. What causes the reflection?

The cause of the image, is the fact that you are in front of the mirror, Therefore, the image inside the mirror is an effect resulting from the cause of you being in front of it. The image is not only an effect, but it is also nonexistent. It is only an illusion.

Who are you?
Are you the *Cause* or the *Effect?*
Who do you want to be?

This Choice, to be the *Cause* or the *Effect*, maybe the MOST IMPORTANT CHOICE YOU MAKE.

What do you want to be? *The cause* or the *effect*

In regards to the important events that will happen in your life, I ask if you would rather be the *cause* or the *effect*. When we allow our impulses to dictate our behavior, we are letting our ego run our lives. Be clear, we have the control to stop our egotistical responses and what happens in our daily lives.

We have programs telling us to get upset when someone cuts in front of us on the freeway and react by giving them the finger. When this happens, we become the *effect* instead of the *cause*. The *effect* took control of our life. We've heard of instances during traffic disputes where one of the people involved pulls out a gun and kills the other. The shooter and the victim's whole life is now ruined because the *effect* (ego) took control instead of the *cause* which is our higher self. Often, we let our ego take control of our lives and push aside our higher self. The higher self always looks at us in disbelief and steps aside with the knowledge that the ego will have to pay for making a decision, a decision that was made like it was driven from a wild and untamed horse. That behavior it's what I refer to as the behavior of the human ego.

The type of behavior described earlier is rooted in our ego, (Lower Self) reacting to an outside event. When we allow it to choose to be the *effect* instead of the *cause*. This *effect* takes control of our life. How many times have we let our ego take control and push aside our higher self without listening to what it says is better for us and for all the parties involved.

> *"Happiness is not a state to arrive at, but a manner of traveling."*
>
> *-Margaret Lee Runbeck-*

I invite you to tame that wild horse by becoming aware (all the time) of the re-actions you take, and choose to stop and think before *reacting*. Take a moment to ask yourself: What is the best choice? Am I going to let my ego react without making a conscious choice? It's like watching a line of dominos set on a table or floor with one piece in front of the other. Sometimes, the process will create beautiful and artistic shapes and forms. When the first one is pushed, it pushes the next one and so on until all the dominos have fallen. There is a chain reaction resulting from the initial "push" or impulse given to only one of the dominoes. We have all heard the phrase that, "he or she pushed my button and I reacted without thinking". How many times has that reaction turned violent and damaged relationships forever or has created painful repercussions for the rest of our lives?

Since ego is the part of you that is capable of hate, my question is: Do you want your ego to run your life? Wouldn't it be better to have your higher self be the *cause* of all your actions; actions that will serve you daily and serve your pursuit of happiness?

In life, we see illusions and think they are real. We believe events that make us unhappy are real and we give values to those events. The values we assign to the events are based on past experiences and programs we've gathered throughout life.

I remember a day in my past, when I was about 12 years old. I was playing with my brother. Then, two friends who lived on our street, came by and invited us in a sneaky way to try and smoke marijuana. The pressure was on. They were good at telling us we were not big enough to even dare to try it. Our egos wanted to react by saying, "I am very macho, I will do it, I am no longer a child." So, what happened is that I decided in the end not to try it. I decided to listen to my higher self. That decision has made a difference in my life up to today.

There is a Native American story in which a young boy is having a conversation with his grandfather. The boy tells his grandfather that he is concerned about which decisions will be correct.

The young boy mentions that he listens to these two wolves constantly fighting inside him. One of the wolves always suggests for him to be lazy and have fun. The same wolf tells him to do bad things like kill animals just for fun and destroy trees and nature. The other wolf on the other hand tells him not to listen to the first wolf; that it is better to be a good boy and to do good for himself and others. That he should be helpful by protecting the weak and by keeping nature clean. The boy is also scared because he will have to confront his fears when he becomes a young warrior and has to spend a night alone in the woods. During that night, he will have to hunt and bring an animal, and by doing that he will be claiming his warrior status. However, one wolf is telling him he will fail and that he is only a scared little boy. The other wolf tells him he is a warrior and he will bring his trophy through a successful hunt night.

> *"The happiness of your life depends upon the quality of your thoughts: therefore, guard accordingly, and take care that you entertain no notions unsuitable to virtue and reasonable nature."*
>
> *-Marcus Aurelius-*

So, the boy asks his grandfather with grave concern, "Grandpa" which wolf is going to win. They are always fighting within my head."

The grandfather looks at his grandson and after a short meditation considering the words he is going to say to his grandchild, calmly answers, "My dear boy, the wolf that is going to win is the one you feed the most." (Author unknown).

Which wolf are you feeding the most? Your ego in the mirror, the reactive side of you? Or, the higher self who knows what is best for you? A beautiful choice to think about; before answering, just become aware and choose wisely.

I recognize that the ego has had a useful part in the evolution of mankind. However, as humanity evolves to be a better race, the ego that served us in the past is dragging us down and slowing the process to become better people. Ego has been the promoter of all war from the beginning of time. The behavior of promoting war in the last 4000 years has obviously not worked. Ego says, you kill one of my soldiers I will kill two of yours; you destroy two of my towers in Manhattan, I will destroy your whole country. It is time for the human race to awaken to better solutions and realize that what we do to others we do to ourselves.

The day after September eleventh, a reporter asked Deepak Chopra, "Mr. Chopra, who do you think was responsible for the attack on the World Trade Center?"

Deepak Chopra after thinking a proper response answered with the following words: "We, we were responsible." and after those words Dr. Deepak Chopra explained his reasoning behind his words.

When you experienced an event early in life that made a negative impact on you, you made a decision to assign specific meaning to that particular event. Later, when similar situations happened again in your life, you repeatedly assigned the same meaning to the new similar event. This happened because the new event reminded you of the original, defining event in your life. You want to validate your first assigned meaning and in order to be "right", you tend to repeat experiences and have similar situations so you can re-validate your ego (yourself) and say, "you see, I was right then and I am right now". How many times have you started a relationship knowing it won't work and then you follow-up with it and eventually you achieve the same results? The programs in your subconscious mind create the same type of events again and again. In other words your ego has to be right and correct.

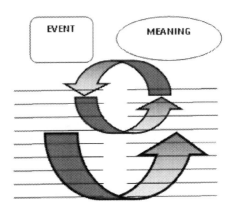

The Meaning of Life

When looking for some answers to the eternal question, "What is the Meaning of Life?" I found a thought that touched me profoundly. I found it in a website with quotes written by Deepak Chopra. He said: -"The Meaning of Life is the progressive expansion of happiness, the ability to have compassion, the ability to Love, to have a sense of connection to the creative source of the Universe which is yourself." -

> *"Religious beliefs are a cover up of insecurity."*
>
> *-Deepak Chopra-*

Fear and suffering comes from separation. The common belief that we are separated from one another is the cause of fear and suffering. We all are *ONE*. Like Deepak Chopra mentions in his statement, "To have a sense of connection to the creative source."

The Course in Miracles lesson 41 of the
workbook says: -**"Depression is an inevitable
consequence of separation."**-

When we choose to believe in separation, we are prone to
depression and suffering. If I choose to be One with everything I
see and everything I don't, I become happy and fear disappears.

Therefore, I suggest you to start being *ONE* with everything,
see yourself in others, (as well as in plants and animals) you are
ONE with everything.

I once took a class at the Landmark Forum. While there, I was
confronted with a reality I didn't like; at the class the facilitator
affirmed that I was a machine and had *"no meaning"*. At first, I
couldn't understand the statement. I refused to accept I had no
meaning at all. The facilitator then demonstrated thoroughly
that what he was claiming was accurate. He proved beyond any
doubt that I was a machine and meaningless, we humans act like
automated machines waking up at the same time, having usually
the same breakfast and meals at the same hours, processing the
food like factories and discarding the food remains on certain
predictable schedule.

I recommend you to take the Landmark Forum. In a few
words, the forum describes that each of us, at an individual level
are meaningless in comparison to the size and complexity of
our solar system, our galaxy and the universe. The entire Earth
is only a tiny speck in the middle of the universe. When I see it
from that perspective, I understand that my life of about 100
years is nothing in comparison to the eternity of the universe,
and *that* is why we are meaningless.

However, the good news is, we can give our lives the meaning
we desire and work on our decision to have the meaning we have
set our life to be.

It is only your choice, a meaning that you like, the meaning that makes you happy and makes the people around you feel blessed in your company.

What meaning do you want to give to your life? Choose a meaning that is worth living. A life full of joy and happiness.

Chapter 3

"Nothing happens until something moves"

-Albert Einstein-

We are all going and/or moving somewhere as long as we are alive. I have said that we always have a choice and that even not choosing is a choice.

However, I want to point out that there are only two things in which we cannot choose. To quote from Terry McBride: "One, we are all going to die, and second, we all must live until we die".

While living, we can choose how we want to feel. We can either choose to be happy or we can choose to be unhappy (depending on what is happening around us). However we can still choose to be happy at any moment and in any circumstance. Therefore, *choose happiness all of the time!*

What is the only thing no one can take from you? The freedom of choice. Life can take away from you, your most precious things, your loved ones, even your limbs. Even so, no one (not even life) can take away your power of choice.

Therefore, you can choose happiness at any time and in any circumstance.

> *"When I went to school, they asked me what I wanted to be when I grew up. I wrote down 'Happy'. They told me I didn't understand the assignment, and I told them they didn't understand life."*
>
> *-John Lennon-*

Do you want to know how? I'll give some tips on how to choose happiness.

It is always **easy** to choose happiness once we become conscious of our reactions.

Think of it this way, whatever we do while we live, will either take us up or down. It begins with how we choose. You and only you, have the power to decide where you want to go; do you want to go up or do you want to go down? Another way to see this concept is to ask yourself, "Do I choose to grow or do I choose to be in decay?" You can go up or be growing mentally and spiritually, or you can go down and be in decay mentally and spiritually. There is no other choice. So I again suggest you to choose wisely.

I am going to tell you a story I learned in a very powerful seminar I took in 2004. That seminar is better known as: People Synergistically Involved (PSI). This is the story. "Socrates was teaching his students. One of them was Plato. Socrates said that he had observed that everything in life had three stages, the first of these he called 'Growth'. Everything started in a very small particle of energy and that particle developed through time and had grown until it reached the second stage which he called 'Stability'. Things remained in that stage for a period of time until finally, it was time for the third stage he called 'Decay'.

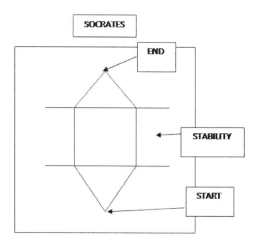

Plato, impressed by his teacher's statement went home meditating on the subject. After spending time and studying the concept he had heard from Socrates, he came to a different conclusion. When Plato went back to Socrates, he explained what he had concluded after meditating on his master's lesson of the three stages: Growth, Stability and Decay. Plato told Socrates he believed the statement had a false premise, which was the second stage "Stability". He (Plato) stated that there was no stability stage, everything was either growing or in decay. They talked and debated regarding the matter and after several hours both came to the conclusion that Plato was correct. There was only growth or decay. The stability stage was an illusion.

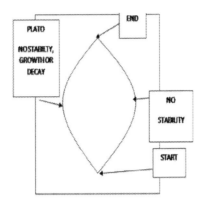

An example of this is when we see a piece of furniture like a chair or a table and we see that it is stable because it takes a lot of time for this piece of furniture to wear out and eventually disappear. However, little by little, the molecules that make up the wood are coming apart and are in a slow but complete decay. Even if we can't see it, it is happening. The same is true of a concrete building. If it is left standing, it could be there for centuries after we are gone (just like the pyramids of Egypt). However little by little the pyramids will be gone one day. They are in decay because they are not growing any more.

When did the wood furniture begin its decay? At the precise moment the tree was cut down.

Taking these thoughts and applying them to our lives, I challenge you to ask yourself, "Am I growing or am I in decay?" Then ask, -What can I do to keep myself growing all the time?- Your subconscious mind will find an answer and will help you to always keep growing.

One way to know if you are in decay, is if you find yourself in a very comfortable place; if you are comfortable, you are probably in a decay stage. *Growth is always outside of the comfort zone.* A baby growing teeth, is not comfortable. A teenager outgrowing his clothes, is not comfortable. A company reaching for new customers and hiring, making decisions and growing, is not comfortable. Usually, comfort equals decay.

This book is about happiness and the choice to be happy. Ask yourself if growing is a better choice for happiness or if decay is a better choice for happiness. What are your responses and your choices?

Be true to yourself.

This chapter began with the quote "Nothing happens until something moves". Are you moving in the GROWTH direction? Are you making choices that will make you a better you? Observe that I wrote a better you, not better than someone else.

I suggest being better than what I am in this moment, that is growth. I can strive to be better than someone else, but if that someone else is far better than me, I will become frustrated with not being equal or better than them or not being able to follow their steps. For example, I can choose to be better than the professional basketball player Michael Jordan. In trying to play better than him I will eventually be frustrated. I will never jump as far and as high, because I am short, overweight, and older. Even so, I can still pursue to be better of what I am now by working on improving my fitness and jumping capabilities by working out and achieving a better body and health. I know it is possible and will be very satisfied through achieving better results than the ones I have now. I am being better than my previous self.

Chapter 4

Being HAPPY just because

What did you think when you read the title of this chapter?

> *"Being Happy, doesn't mean that everything is perfect. It means that you've decided to look beyond the imperfections"*
>
> *-Unknown-*

I chose the title for this chapter thinking that there is no specific reason for being happy. Throughout life, we may go through stages and events that will make us happy due to the nature of the event. I think that because we have experienced happiness due to these special events, we are always expecting to have special events that will trigger our happiness.

So, most of the time we are waiting for **an event** to be happy. Let me tell you something very important. **The important event is now,** each moment of your life is the **important event** you are waiting for. Therefore, we can choose to be happy **now**, not in the future, **now**; in this very moment, without stopping to analyze if **now** is the right moment to be happy or not, just **be happy** now.

How about just **being happy for no reason**, wouldn't that be awesome? The fact is, we all can choose to **be happy for no reason at all**. Our minds have been programmed to think that happiness is always related to an external event that is good or satisfying to our beliefs and programs. Therefore, it is a subjective value that we put on the event that makes us happy.

> *"Happiness is the art of never holding in your mind the memory of any unpleasant thing that has passed."*
>
> *-Unknown-*

So if all events are seen with different eyes and different programs that we can call good or bad, what if **we choose to be happy without qualifying any event and just be happy for no reason?** The key is to stop waiting for something to happen according to our subjective perception of an event as the true reality that will make us happy. Any circumstance and any moment are ideal to feel happy if we choose to feel happiness.

> *"Folks are usually about as happy as they make their minds up to be."*
>
> *-Abraham Lincoln-*

Do you think that you can do that?

Did I made my point?

We can all be happy just because. We do not need a reason, we do not need a special event, we do not need drugs or alcohol, and we do not need a special person who will make us happy. We simply need to make a decision, a very important decision that will change our lives, a decision to be happy all of the time.

Chapter 5

The power of a SMILE

While I was studying Neurolinguistic Programming, one of the facts I learned, was the fact that our body recognizes the postures we assume and the faces we make. Then, it reacts to them and literally puts our bodies into that state.

> -*"Sometimes your joy is the source of your smile, but sometimes your smile can be the source of your joy."*-
>
> -*Thich Nhat Hanh*-

Would you like to do an experiment right now? I invite you to do this, and you will be amazed.

It will take no more than five minutes and I assure you it will prove that anyone can change the way they feel, either one way or the other way. Do not believe what I am saying; do the exercise and see what happens. That way you won't believe me, you will believe in you and your results.

This experiment goes like this:

1. Be in a standing position
2. Close your eyes

3. Think about a moment in your past where you experienced sadness, discomfort, pain. For example; the passing of a loved one, the death of a pet, being fired from a job or another experience, like a physical pain. Feel the feelings you had at that moment; see the scenes you were experiencing then, like it is happening right now. Experience the bright colors, and listen to the sounds, words and noises that were spoken or present in that very moment. What were your feelings of pain? Where did it hurt the most? Re-live the moment as if it were right where you are now listening to the words, watching the people and re-living the feelings that were present in that moment of your past. Now, be conscious of how you feel and the status of your body and posture. How are your muscles, your limbs? What is the position of your head? What is going through your mind and how do you feel right now as you remember that sad, ugly moment of your past? Notice your body. How are your arms and legs positioned? How is your breathing? Shallow or deep? How are your back and torso positioned?

Notice your feelings. I can assure you that if you are following the instructions, by now you are feeling sad. However keep reading.

Did you notice the posture of your body and head? What is happening in your thoughts and mind? Nothing pleasant, I assume.

Some people report, that their shoulders are down, their eyes also are looking down, probably their back is slightly bent forward and their lips are in a inverted "U" position.

4. Now, let's keep with the experiment and see what is going to happen next.

Next, I want you to be in the same standing position: remove yourself from remembering the painful moment from the past. Turn your head up, look upward, raise your shoulders and smile. Now think of a pleasurable moment, a moment of joy and happiness where you were the center of attention and everybody is telling you how great you are: listen to their words. Feel the joy of that moment now. Everyone is cheering for you up, everyone is impressed by something you have done or achieved, and everyone is happy for you and they are all congratulating you for the achievement, keep your shoulders up and straight, your head lifted up.

I want you to see upward. (your eyes looking at the ceiling or above if you are in an open space area). I want you to start jumping with both feet up in the air as high as you can! Stop jumping! Now, be in a standing position and look above. I want you to feel what you were experiencing in that moment. Everybody was congratulating you. I want you to listen to the words they were saying to you or about you. I want you to remember your laughter and the feelings of joy and happiness. I want you to see the place you were. The bright colors, the faces laughing and the people happy for you, the place and the scenery. See it all as if it is happening right now. And listen to the sounds from your memory of that precise moment and feel what you were feeling that day. That beautiful day in which you were being congratulated, noticed and recognized. Feel it now.

Notice what is happening to your body. Notice your facial expression. Are you smiling? What does your body feel? What is the position of your head? Your arms? Your legs and your chest? What is going through your mind in this very moment? Be aware of your feelings. Bring that memory of joy and happiness into the here and now and feel exactly the same again. Start jumping! Scream loud! Laugh loudly! Say: *I AM HAPPY! I AM HAPPY! I AM*

HAPPY! Your body is now generating endorphins and you surely are feeling joyful and happy!

If the experiment went as I expected (and as I have experienced through many of my seminars), you were able to change your feelings from sadness to joy and happiness in a matter of minutes. Didn't you?

You probably are feeling happy thoughts and happy sensations. Some people even say that they feel chills on their arms, and start laughing for no reason.

The object of this exercise is to demonstrate that it is possible to change your mood and feelings easily and fast as we just did. The only thing required was your decision to follow the instructions for the exercise. If you did, I have just made my point that being happy is a decision we can all make, at any moment.

Now, notice that the pain you had a few minutes ago has changed. You went from being comfortable reading these words, to a moment of pain that you remembered and then back to a moment of joy (that you also remembered). The pain you felt has disappeared. In a few moments, you were able to change your feelings and your body postures by **choice** simply by following my instructions. Was it hard? No. You just chose to follow my instructions and it was easy. I can tell you that to be happy all the time is as easy as this exercise. You can choose to be happy but only if you choose to do so.

The posture of your body helps. The brain knows that in order to be sad, you have to have a sad position of your body. (head down shoulders down, column and upper body bent forward, sad face, looking down). The most important thing is thinking sad or bad thoughts. Your body's posture helps you to feel happy and healthy. Put your shoulders up and back and put your spine straight. Look up with your eyes and smile. Walk with energetic steps and think happy and funny thoughts. Your body will recognize the posture and will immediately generate endorphins that will change your body's well being and make it healthier. As you can see with this exercise, it is very easy and it is a choice.

Now the question is: Will you choose to do this exercise each morning? Just do the second part, and choose to be happy.

> -"*True happiness comes from the joy of deeds well done, the zest of creating things new.*"-
>
> -*Antoine de Saint-Exupery*-

This is the power of your body's position and the memories in all the cells of your body. If you decide to change only the position of your body and smile, you will be feeling happy all the time. At first, you may have to work at it. Maybe it will require some effort, and little by little it will become easier. You will experience happiness all of the time. You will be in control of how you want to feel at any time.

This exercise is an example of the power we have to change our thoughts and the focus of our attention. If we choose to live and focus only in the present moments, we will have no pain. If we have pain, it is due to a present circumstance. It might be muscular pain due to exercise, or mental pain due to losing a loved one. The pain only exists in the past. Let me make a correction; there is another kind of pain: The pain from thinking of the future. It is based on worries or presumptions about something that it may never happen.

> *-"I am determined to be cheerful and happy in whatever situation I may find myself. For I have learned that the greater part of our misery or unhappiness is determined not by our circumstance but by our disposition."-*
>
> *-Martha Washington-*

There are studies that prove that it takes fewer muscles to smile than it takes to frown, so the fact is that you will be spending less energy by being happy and smiling rather than being sad or upset.

The power of BELIEFS.

Now let's talk about the power of a belief: How many times have we heard athletes talk about their success in their sport due to their own belief? They never doubted they would be the greatest in their field. Whether a 100 meters run in less than 10 seconds, or the best basket-ball player like Michael Jordan or Lebron James, or race car drivers who won the championship of their sport. Many just talk about how strongly and surely they believed they would do it. They did it. Many of them practiced in their minds and saw what they believed would happen and they made it happen.

I read a story about Henry Ford that goes something like this: Henry Ford wanted more power for the engines of his cars. He called his team of engineers and asked them to design and build an eight cylinder engine. At the time, Ford's cars were powered by four cylinder engines. He just thought that if he could make an engine double the cylinder, it would have more power. The engineers went to work on a design for a new engine and after a few weeks, they brought plans and told Mr. Ford they had designed an eight cylinder engine in line, one cylinder after the other.

He took a look at the plans and immediately told the engineers that their design would not work. That their engine was too long and would not fit in the front of the car. The car would have to be modified to a longer front hood. The idea was not to Mr. Ford's liking. So, he told them to go back and make a shorter engine with eight cylinders. The engineers went back and after a few days, they returned stating it was impossible to make a shorter engine with eight cylinders.

Mr. Ford asked the group of engineers: "Whoever thinks it is not possible, please move to the left. Those who think it is possible, move to the right". We don't know if he fired the ones who didn't think it was possible, but what we know is that he sent the ones that BELIEVED it was possible to work on the project. Mr. Ford told the group of engineers the following: -"If you believe you can, or if you believe you cannot, you are right. You either can or cannot." That is the power of belief.

You can either be happy or can't be happy according to your personal beliefs.

> -*"My happiness grows in direct proportion to my acceptance, and in inverse proportion to my expectations."*-
>
> - *Michael J. Fox-*

Our beliefs are based on personal experiences since the day we were born. As I said before, we are the sum of our experiences and the way we think and react to any circumstance, our behavior is always determined by our past experiences. These create the total sum of our beliefs. You might ask. "If those were my experiences and I behave according to my past experiences, how am I going to be happy with all the things that have happened to me?" My suggestion is to think about the possibility of a new start from scratch.

Imagine you just had an accident and you were hit in your head and because of that, you don't remember anything that happened to you. You are a clean slate. So, nothing from your past will determine how you feel or act. Start anew. Create happy moments and happy events. You just have to imagine them, it is that easy. Your beliefs are what you are and you can change your beliefs at will.

The power of a belief is described in the Bible in Mark 11:23 and Matthew 21:21. In the passage where it says that if we have faith as of the size of a grain of mustard, we can say to a mountain: "Move!" and the mountain will move. That is the power of faith, and the power of our beliefs.

In one of Deepak Chopra's books, he writes about the placebo effect and its counterpart nocebo effect. He mentions a personal experience with a doctor he befriended. His friend used to smoke a great deal and his coworkers suggested he stop smoking. After several years of being told to quit, the doctor decided to take an X-ray of his lungs. When he saw his own X-rays, he found a small spot he believed was cancer and was sure he was going to die soon. A few weeks later became very ill and died. Since Dr. Deepak Chopra was his friend, the Management at the hospital asked Dr. Chopra to pick up all his deceased friend's belongings from his office. When Dr. Chopra was going through his belongings, he found an old X-ray study dated 20 years earlier when his friend applied for the job at the hospital. To Dr. Chopra's surprise, the x-ray showed the same spot in the same place and of the same size of the spot of the new x-rays that his friend believed to be cancer. He had the same spot 20 years earlier and never had any health problems.

In all those 20 years the Doctor didn't pay attention to the spot in his lungs, he went on with his life as if he was perfectly healthy.

The power of belief killed this doctor. Since he was a doctor, he knew and believed he would die and so he did.

I invite you to believe you can be happy. Just because.

In the last chapter you'll receive 365 affirmations of happiness. You can repeat one each day for a year and a new program of happiness and joy will be programmed in your subconscious mind. You will be happy all the time if you choose to follow the challenge of reading and repeating throughout the day an affirmation for 365 days.

Chapter 6

Formulas that help the habit for Happiness Creation

This is what has been missing until now! some concise and actionable steps that would help you bring happiness into your life and make happiness a constant daily feeling of Joy.

> -"*Disease cannot live in a body that's in a healthy emotional state.*"-
>
> -*Bob Proctor*-

Many people are far from being content with their lives the way they are in this moment, with what they have, and usually people are constantly pushing themselves to acquire more stuff and seek validation from others. When I realized this pattern of behavior, I concluded that for some reason people value more the opinion of others than their own opinion. People buy cars, because their neighbors bought a new car, they want to keep up with the people around them or be better than them, maybe trying to feel superior to others.

When each one of us realizes that we are a divine creation that is a resemblance of the divine, then we will not require the validation of others for believing in ourselves. Or need to have more than the others to be worthy.

The Importance of Choosing Happiness

Happy feelings come from happy thoughts, which in turn produce more effective and joyful actions, habits and outcomes. Because of these actions, Happiness seems to have magical powers. Some scientists claim it can make people healthier, even live longer and also become more creative.

I'm sure you've wondered why some people live happier lives than others. The answer is simple: they have developed a program in their subconscious mind, a certain way of thinking, and they choose to be Happy. They somehow found the co-relation between their thoughts and their results.

Andrew Steptoe, Psychology Professor at University College London, claims that happier people have lower chances of suffering from things like heart disease and stroke. The explanation is simple: happier people have better health habits, stronger immune system and also endure pain better.

According to a recent study from The University of North Carolina, psychologists discovered that people who spice their lives with positivity, can cope better against bad situations and protect themselves from stress.

So, it is definitely well worth bringing more happy feelings into your life.

Recently, I heard on the television a study of the areas in the whole world, where people live over a hundred years, they called these areas, the blue areas of the world. One of the things that the people who live in these areas, is that they practice been happy most of the time, some mentioned that the way they did it, was by accepting what it was, or as some put it; by surrendering to what happens.

Here is a series of formulas or steps, I gathered from different sources, that can help you restore happiness all around you and others in your environment, and guide you toward a much more fulfilling life:

Become Aware of the Way You are Thinking.

Most people live by default and only react to what is going on around them. Your thoughts generate your feelings, so you may want to choose your thoughts carefully. Every time you find yourself dwelling upon a negative thought, weed it out by replacing it with its positive counterpart.

How to choose happiness at any time?

Happiness is a state of mind, you cannot find it outside yourself. You don't need to have a lot of time or go somewhere special to be at peace and revel in a moment of happiness. Gratitude is the easiest way to shift from negative vibes and feel happy again.

Every time you feel down, stop for a moment and really count your blessings. Feel the blessings coming from the things you already have and see yourself living a happy and healthy lifestyle. Never forget that someone somewhere is happy with less than what you have.

Let Happiness Guide You.

Can you choose happiness at any time? Yes, you can! Famous psychiatrist and Holocaust-survivor Viktor Frankl said: "The one thing you can't take away from me is the way I choose to respond to what you do to me. The last of one's freedoms is to choose one's attitude in any given circumstance."

So you are the captain of your own ship, which is your mind. No one can force you to think or feel anything that you don't want. Things happen all the time. Instead of focusing on what you don't want, choose to see the exact opposite of worry, anxiety and the negative. Enjoy your moments of gratitude, be thankful for who you are and what is, and tap into your own source of happiness and love.

Plus, happier people attract what they want faster. Powerful emotions help increase your power of attraction. When visualizing your dream life, feel the joy, happiness and excitement as if the object of your desire is already yours. The stronger your emotions, the faster you can manifest.

Analyze what is more important and set priorities.

Psychologist Ed Diener claims there is no single key to happiness, but rather a mix of ingredients. The ingredients mainly are: A) Healthy social relationships, B) Worthy goals and C) A purpose in life.

We, as humans, are able to define our top priority areas and nourish them with our love and attention. Then, we focus on what has value for us and the satisfaction of being present and doing what is important to us. The sole fact of doing this, brings happiness and satisfaction.

For most people, family and friends come first. Scientists agree that just as stress can damage our immune system, friendship and happiness can protect our bodies. According to research, the healthy benefits of marriage can add an average of seven years to the life of a man and about four for a woman.

Surround yourself with people who will support your thoughts and ideas. This by itself, will lift you higher. Surround yourself with happy, positive people, those who truly want the best for you and your loved ones, people who will support you in your desires and dreams, people who accept you as you are and will not want you to change to fit their perception of their world.

Meditate.

Every day new studies show that meditation has great benefits on health and well-being. It increases positive emotions, immune function and life satisfaction. It also brings calm to your life, and people will notice your new way of being that says you are enlightened.

Do what you love.

You will be surprised to realize that more than 90% of people do not do on a daily basis what they love, they do what life throws at them. A majority of people dislike their jobs. Choose to do something that you enjoy and make time in your schedule for your hobbies and to pursue your very special desires and interests.

Laugh often.

This is great advice; just laugh for no reason, be crazy and be happy. Dr. Kataria started the laughter club in India and now there are laughter clubs all around the world. People go to these meetings just to laugh for no reason. Their health improves and their lives get better, people live longer just by laughing, studies prove that people get healed just by laughing. Don't take life too seriously. Laugh at yourself, laugh at your circumstances and infuse fun into daily activities.

Practice forgiveness.

Jesus said, "Forgive them because they do not know what they are doing" Holding onto anger, resentment or jealousy will only hurt you. Learn to say:

"So what?, Now, what"

forgive others and forgive yourself for anything in your past that keeps haunting you in your consciousness. Let it go and create a new now and a better future by choice.

Stop comparing.

Every time there is a comparison, one of the compared sides will be less or negative. Avoid the possibility of seeing two or more outcomes. Happy people don't waste their time worrying about what could or should have happened, they do not pay attention to what other people think, nor do they gossip.

There is a story about Socrates author unknown, that goes like this:

-"In ancient Greece, Socrates was reputed to hold knowledge in high esteem. One day an acquaintance met the great philosopher and said, 'Socrates, do you know what I just heard about your friend?'

'Hold on a minute,' Socrates replied. 'Before telling me anything I'd like you to pass a little test. It's called the Triple Filter Test.'

'Triple filter?' Said the acquaintance.

'That's right,' Socrates continued. 'Before you talk to me about my friend, it might be a good idea to take a moment and filter what you're going to say. The first filter is Truth. Have you made absolutely sure that what you are about to tell me is true?'

'No, the man said, actually I just heard about it and...'

'All right,' said Socrates. 'So you don't really know if it's true or not. Now let's try the second filter, the filter of Goodness. Is what you are about to tell me about my friend something good?'

'No, on the contrary...'

'So,' Socrates continued, 'you want to tell me something bad about him, but you're not certain it's true. You may still pass the test though, because there's one filter left: the filter of Usefulness. Is what you want to tell me about my friend going to be useful to me?'

'No, not really.'

'Well,' concluded Socrates, 'if what you want to tell me is neither true nor good nor even useful, why tell it to me at all?'

This is why Socrates was a great philosopher and held in such high esteem."-

Let go of the need to judge or criticize. Instead, concentrate on creating and living **your** best you and your best life.

Love.

It's been said that God is Love. When we focus on being a loving person, we are acting like we are that quality of God, therefore becoming like God. When we are like God, we radiate happiness and joy. Nurture your relationships, friends and family with loving actions and attitude, and make it a priority to spend time with and to support your loved ones.

Keep learning.

Authors Chris Brady and Orrin Woodward, in their book *"Launching a Leadership Revolution"*, mention that human beings gradually forget what they know. As they write *"If we do not know what we do not know, and if we are gradually forgetting what we do know, it will probably be a good idea to continue learning; that way at least we will know something!"*

Invest time and energy into continually learning and developing new skills. Keep your brain stimulated with exciting information and hobbies.

Be positive.

I used to tell my kids that when we are born, it is like we come into life in a certain place like on a school ruler. Rulers have little marks that measure sixteenths of an inch and eighths of an inch; these marks in a ruler let us know if we are in the same place or if we are moving. We always have a choice where to move. We either move to one side or the other side of the ruler; one side we inherently know is the correct side to move forward to, the other side we could call the negative side.

The fact is that we have to move in life, we are not supposed to stay in the same place, so choose to which side you want to move, either to a more positive side or to a more negative side; you inherently know which side is better for you. Start moving towards what makes you happier. Make an effort to see the glass half full, and always look for the silver lining in any situation. If you notice that a negative thought is creeping into your mind, counteract it with a powerful, positive affirmation.

Appreciate life.

Enjoy all your time, enjoy every moment of your life. Although there are actually very small moments of time where people suffer a loss or pain, most of the time we can choose the feeling of being happy, being great.

The word great has the same root as being grateful. Develop an attitude of gratitude and count your blessings. When you start looking for things to be thankful for, you'll discover more reasons to be happy. Gratefulness creates happiness.

Chapter 7

Eden, the promised Paradise

In all religious traditions we find a common denominator; they each have the belief in a place of eternal joy and happiness. All religions aim to reach that place of joy and they promise everyone that if people follow their rules, they will reach that place of eternal Joy.

What if that place of eternal joy is right here and now in front of you, without the need for religion in order to be in that place of joy and happiness? The only thing you need in order to reach that promised joy and happiness is a very simple action. The action of choice! Choose to be in a state of joy and happiness all the time.

Through my personal thoughts and experience, I found that fear and suffering comes from separation. The common belief that we are separated from one another is what causes fear and suffering. Have you heard of the concept that "we all are ONE"?

In the Course in Miracles Workbook, lesson 41 says:

"Depression is an inevitable consequence of separation".

When we choose to believe in separation, we are prone to depression and suffering.

If I choose to be one with everything I see, and everything I do not see, then it is easy to become happy.

You might ask: Why will I be happy if I choose to think I am one with everything? How am I going to be one with what I do not see? I am sitting here in my chair and there are six and a half billion people all over the world. I can't be one with all those people.

> *"The World is only in the Mind of its maker."*
>
> *-A course in Miracles-*

If you just see the physical evidence of your body, you won't be able to think you are one with all. However, consider this: are you a human being having a spiritual experience or are you a spiritual being having a human experience? As a spiritual being, you were never born and you will never die. We are all made of atoms, energy; everyone is the same. Rocks are also made out of atoms and energy; the very bricks of our being, are the same for all humanity and all things in the universe. We are all One, made out of the same stuff.

I think all human beings have had the experience of fear or at least understand the concept of fear. What is fear? What is the origin of fear? Why do we fear?

I took a Kabbalah course and learned that we have two natures. One nature is that we are **proactive** and the other nature is that we are also **reactive**. Once I understood the concept of being **reactive** and **proactive** I concluded that the **reactive** nature is the **ego** driven force. The **reactive** nature identifies itself with the **ego**, and it is the nature that helps us to survive and thrive. Our bodies keep us alive and defend us from possible threats. In a civilization like ours, the United States of America, we don't usually need the acute survival skill of fight or flight. However, we still have the reptilian brain inside which is responsible for controlling the survival forces in us. We **react**, to things like someone in the freeway crossing our lane and become furious. We begin road rage behaviors all because of our **reactive** nature. This doesn't help our evolution as a species. Even so, it is embedded in us from our past.

On the other hand, we have the **proactive** nature that identifies itself with **our higher self**, the **spiritual** side of us. The proactive nature doesn't **react**, but has a great deal of patience and stops before reacting and **thinks** before acting. Often times it just waits. Once the **reactive** nature has jumped and reacted, it will occur either violently or in a mood that eventually will back-fire on us.

The **reactive** nature is one driven by **fear.** Our **egos** are there to protect us from dying and from getting hurt. However, there are good news and bad news. All of our bodies are going to die some day. The **ego** knows this fact and is terrified of it. *That* is the origin of fear. On the other side, the **Higher self or Spiritual self,** (as I said before) was never born and will never die, and therefore does not know fear. Who do you want to be in control of your life?

Do you want your **ego** to keep reacting to circumstances, or do you want to let **your Higher self** take control of your life? I have asked this question of many people and all say the same thing, "I want to have my higher self control my life." My response to them is that is easy to say the words, and then I invite them to really live by what they said.

How can they do it? It is **easy.** Just live in the now by being aware of who you are.

How do you become aware? Only by being **conscious** at all times. In a passage of the Bible it says: "Pray without ceasing." What does the phrase mean? It doesn't mean to repeat a prayer 24/7. It actually means to **be conscious at all times; be aware of who you are, a Spiritual Being, having a human experience.**

The Action of CHOICE.

Let's think about this question, Can we consciously choose to be joyful and happy at any moment in time? The key word here is **consciously**; the answer is **yes**. Happiness and Joy is always a choice. It does not matter what is happening around us. It is always what we make out of what is happening around us that makes us either happy or unhappy. It is the inner personal interpretation of any particular event, occurring at any moment that determines whether we are **happy, sad, mad or miserable.**

What is the quality of your choices regarding your personal interpretation of the events around you in each moment of your day? Is there a person in your work place that triggers certain feelings, either of joy or discomfort?

Do you realize that when you start experiencing those feelings as soon as you see that person, it has nothing to do with them? It is all about how your subconscious mind controls your feelings when you observe an external event. Your perception of someone in front of you or the way a person acts or reacts to another event, is just a reaction from the programs embedded in your subconscious through the personal experiences of your life.

> *"Insanity; is to expect different results doing the same things we have always done."*
>
> -Albert Einstein-

The way you **react** and the way you think are the sum of the experiences that have created programs in your subconscious mind. You are a product of your experiences. If you had different experiences, you would be a different person.

The realization that we are in control of our feelings and emotions is what will set us free and bring us to that promised paradise or Eden right here and now. Imagine if you could choose to be happy all the time?

Will that be the state of mind we are all are aiming for? Each of us at any moment, can be in Paradise or Eden by choice. That is what all religious philosophies have always said. We just misinterpreted their words.

Do you know that you have a choice on how your reaction can develop? It is all about the choices each of us have each moment. The **choice to be happy** is the choice that was meant to be. When the Bible talks about the Tree of Knowledge, and the aftermath of eating the fruit of the tree of knowledge, it means that at every moment, we have the consciousness of choice, **the knowledge of choice.**

Since that biblical or historical moment, some of us have made the choice of separation and competition. That is why certain populations see themselves as different from others and that they have the "truth" while others do not. We created the idea of separation and the idea that, "I am right and you wrong". This process of thought creates envy, hate and mayhem.

> *"There is only one way to happiness and that is to cease worrying about things which are beyond the power of our will."*
>
> -Epictetus-

On the other hand, I invite you to make a different choice, the choice of unification and cooperation. I suggest that the difference in the choices certainly will bring in your life a different outcome, one of joy and abundance. If you do not like the life you have created, guess what? You have a choice to change it. How? By changing your perception of the events around you.

Wayne Dyer in many of his public talks, has said the following statement: "When I change the way I see things, the things I see change." If you want to change your life, change the way you see the things around you. If we do not change, the things we perceive and create are going to be the same things we have created so far. As previously quoted Albert Einstein said:

> **"Insanity is to expect different results doing the same things we have always done."**

When we consciously choose happiness, we are in that Eden or Paradise that all religions mention and that we all aim to reach one day. You can be there right **now**. Just **choose** happiness instead of mayhem at any moment of your life. Always remember it is a **choice** and that any **choice** can be changed at any moment as easy as counting one, two, three.

Any **choice** is as easy or difficult as each of us decides to believe it is. The same **choice** can be easy for one person and difficult for another. What makes the difference is the perception of difficulty and of the **choice** by each of us. If the **choice** and outcome are the same for anyone, what makes it seem more difficult or easer is the way we each perceive it to be.

I invite each of you reading this book to choose, to make your life easy, to enjoy and to be happy and joyful. Remember that the outcome each of us creates is in direct relationship to our beliefs.

We attract what we are. We create around us what we believe we will have and finally, we have today what we have always wanted.

Sometimes we say we want something different than what we have today. However, based on the results, what we have today is what we have always wanted, no more no less. Look at what you have in your bedroom. Did you select that bed? Did you choose the color of the curtains? Did you choose that toothbrush at the store? Did you choose to work for the company you work for today or did you choose to have the business you have today? We all have what we have created by our own choices.

Look at everything that there is in your life today and ask yourself honestly if you somehow chose to have what you have in your life. Nobody put a pistol in your head and forced you to have what you have. You, yourself, settled for what you have knowing that you could have maybe other even better things.

Now is the time for you to start making different choices regarding your outcome and happiness. Now that you know that what you have is because you decide to have what you have, the question is: Are you satisfied with what you have? Do you want to change it?

If you want to change what you have created. remember the fantabulous gift I gave you in chapter one.

You might think: Oh! But it is so difficult to go for what I really want! So remember that there is a proven way that you can use to overcome your old way of thinking. Whenever you desire something that might seem difficult to achieve; just repeat to yourself the following affirmations that are very effective for changing your subconscious mind:

**"YES I CAN!
IT IS EASY!
I AM DOING IT NOW!"**

"YES I CAN; IT IS EASY, AND I AM DOING IT."

these words every day of your life, in the morning, ne, before going to sleep, and every time you have to do something that you think will be difficult.

These three sentences repeated every day and every time you remember or wish to remember, will make a big difference in how your subconscious mind will approach the work it has to do for you to achieve what you want. The subconscious mind is our slave and will do anything we tell it to do; so, when you issue the command "YES I CAN," your subconscious mind will start working on your command that says "I CAN DO IT," here the important issue is to avoid giving other orders that counteract the original order. Saying "IT IS EASY", is highly important because what you say to your subconscious mind, will determine your results. Do you want the change to be easy, or will you give ambivalent orders that will make it not so easy? Again, that is your choice. **Choose wisely.**

I want to end this chapter by welcoming you to your New Eden or Paradise by your own choice. You can stay where you are, re-creating what you have created, by choosing your ongoing and desired actual way of life. Or you can try something new and powerful to create what you really desire for yourself.

Will you choose paradise or hell? Whichever you choose, **welcome to your life.**

Chapter 8

The importance of the words I AM

The "I AM"

Are you willing to accept a challenge? I invite you to make a better use of the words "I AM".

How do you use the words "I AM"? Can you say to yourself: "*I AM HAPPY* every single day and every single moment of your life?" I say that happiness is a choice, so my question to you is: can you fake it till you make it? And start saying to yourself whenever you remember: "*I AM HAPPY?*" Maybe you could set the alarm of your watch, and when you hear the chime each hour, say to yourself: "*I AM HAPPY!*", and do it as often as possible.

Use your imagination and recall moments in which you were happy. Your body will immediately recognize those memories and generate endorphins in your system that will alter the status of your body, creating automatic happiness, just by you thinking happy thoughts. At first it will cost you certain effort, however with time and practice, it will be second nature to be happy all the time.

> "Creative Imagination is not something reserved for the poets,
> the philosophers, the inventors. It enters into our every act.
> For imagination sets the goal 'picture' which our automatic
> mechanism works on. We act, or fail to act, not because of
> 'will,' as is so commonly believed, but because of imagination."
>
> -Maxwell Maltz-

I want to express the importance of the words **"I AM.** "Let me paraphrase a passage of the Bible that relates to the moment in which Moses heard a voice coming from a burning bush on the side of the mountain. He heard a request from the voice, telling him to go back to Egypt and talk to Pharaoh in order to request the freedom of the Jews from bondage.

Moses was perplexed. He was expelled from Egypt by the pharaoh who was now his enemy. However, he knew that he must obey the voice from the burning bush. He had doubts and asked why him, since he is not a good speaker, (He used to stutter, so he didn't have confidence in himself). He was attempting to avoid the issue and asked the voice, "Who shall I tell Pharaoh is sending me with this crazy request? "He asked the voice, **"What is your name?"** and the voice from the burning bush responds;

"I AM THAT I AM"

These powerful words in English, are the name of God as per the scriptures. The words in Hebrew are written from right to left as follows: Hay -Vav-Hay -Yud - (HVHY).

God's Name is the four-letter name represented by the Hebrew letters Yud-Hay-Vav-Hay (YHVH). In certain dictionaries, it is often referred to as the "Ineffable Name", the "Unutterable Name" or the "Distinctive Name". Linguistically, it is related to the Hebrew root Hay-Yud-Hay (to be), and reflects the fact that God's existence is eternal.

In Hebrew these letters sound something like: "YUD HAY VAV HAY". Those Hebrew letters mean, *"I AM THAT I AM".* If we listen closely to the sound of the letters which have been forbidden to be spoken in the Hebrew religion, it would sound altogether like, "Jehovah or Yehova" which is the name of God in the bible. What I want to point out here, is; that Jehovah is not a name. It is a statement from God, saying that his name is, *"I AM".*

So, knowing this; each of us should be very careful of the words we put after each *"I AM"* because every time we say *"I AM"* with our mouth and within our thoughts and put an image of us or a word that we think describes us, after those words, we are actually invoking the name and presence of **God** and asking or praying that the words after our *"I AM"* become a reality with the approval of **GOD.** We are asking for a confirmation of our statement of the words we said after our *"I AM".*

So if I say, "I am beautiful "God says, yes you are. If I say, "I am powerful", "the universe says", "Yes you are". If I say, "I am shy", "the whole universe conspires for you" to be that way. This works for any other word you say after your *"I AM's."* I invite you to say, *"I AM HAPPY"* all the time, and do it by choice.

What will you start saying once you accept this awesome truth? What are you're *I AM's* going to be from now on?

"I AM" is the name of **all** names and you; believe it or not, **you are** a part of the **UNIVERSAL "I AM"**

The name we all use, all the time without really thinking the immense power that lies in the words *"I AM".* I invite you to start paying attention, each time you speak the words *"I AM"* and what you put after the words.

Start saying *I AM HAPPY EVERY DAY*, because whatever words you put after your *I AMs*, will be supported and backed up by the **UNIVERSE, GOD** or whatever you call the **SOURCE** or the tremendous force that created the entire Universe.

The funder of PSI Seminars, Thomas Willhite, explained this concept in a particular way, he used to say that our "I AM's" can put us in a small jail or takes us to unlimited places, the concept of "I AM" is infinite and it will always produce what we attach to our "I AM's" It is our own creation the fact that we can put limited or unlimited beliefs to our "I AM"

I AM POWERFUL
IAM BEAUTIFUL
IAM INTELIGENT
I AM SMART
I AM AWESOME
I AM LEARNING EVERY DAY
I AM HEALTHY
I AM HAPPY
I AM WHOLE
I AM UNIQUE
I AM LOVED
I AM LOVE
I AM SPECIAL
I AM RICH
I AM WEALTHY
I AM .... you put your own words

I AM, THAT I AM.
YUD HAY VAV HAY

Note: The Hebrew and Yiddish languages use a different alphabet than English. The picture in the next page illustrates the Hebrew alphabet, in Hebrew alphabetical order. Note that Hebrew is written from right to left, rather than left to right as in English, so Aleph is the first letter of the Hebrew alphabet and Tav is the last. The Hebrew alphabet is often called the "alefbet," because of its first two letters.

Letters of the Alefbet. Hebrew is read from right to left, see the letters below, from right to left.

You can look at the Hebrew letters and listen the pronunciation of YOD HEI VAV HEI in Wikipedia at the following link:

http://en.wikipedia.org/wiki/Tetragrammaton

Hebrew	Letter name	Pronunciation
י	Yodh	[j]
ה	He	[h]
ו	Waw	[w]

(or placeholder for "O"/"U" vowel, see mater lectionis)

ה	He	[h]

(or often a silent letter at the end of a word)

If you believe in a supreme force of *God*, just think that when that superior force or *God* decided to create the universe, and *God* was all that existed at the time, just ask yourself:

"Where did *God*, get all matter in order to create the universe if the only thing that existed was *God* itself?" Well, the answer is easy. In order to create everything in the universe and all that exists even though you do not see it, **God** created everything out of **ITSELF**. Everything is and has been created out of **GOD's** energy. You and I and all six and a half billion people are made and are part of **God**, as all matter, freeways, buildings, seas and oceans, animals and planets and galaxies, all of them are made out of **God** stuff.

That is why I affirm we are all one, and not only one with each other, we all are **ONE WITH GOD**. Once you understand and digest it, then you will be able to let go of fear and welcome happiness as a choice. Then, and only then, fear disappears.

Everything that exists, everything we see and everything we do not see, everything we experience or not, is made out of that **unique and only conscious energy.** So, **EVERYTHING** is made out of **GOD STUFF**, or **GOD CONSCIOUSNESS.**

Einstein said, "Energy cannot be created neither destroyed, it can only be transformed." All is energy. The same energy of the source. The paper you are reading from, the chair you are sitting on, the floor that you are stepping on, the windows that you see around you, the car you drove earlier, the pavement it was rolling on, the stop lights and the other cars as well as each and every person you have spoken to in your life and every animal or insect you have seen or experienced. **ALL IS MADE OF GOD STUFF, GOD ENERGY.**

Therefore, **YOU ARE GOD STUFF**, too.

Can you now understand this fact? You are made of **God** stuff, therefore you are part of **God.**

Fear and suffering comes from separation. Joy and happiness exist within being **ONE** with **God** and the Universe.

You are the **"I AM" I AM, THAT I AM.**

If you are having a hard time grasping these concepts, I highly recommend you to read the book called *"The Impersonal Life"* written by **Joseph S. Brenner.**

Matthew 6:22 is the twenty-second verse of the sixth chapter of the Gospel of Matthew in the New Testament, and is part of the Sermon on the Mount. In the King James Version of the Bible the text reads: **The light of the body is the eye: if therefore thine eye be single, thy whole body shall be full of light.**

What it means by "single" is really the capability of seeing *ONENESS* in all.

Chapter 9

Working on your happiness with a Mirror

Working on your happiness with a mirror

When I was in my mid-twenties, I read Louise Hay's book <u>You Can Heal Your Life</u>. Louise Hay works very effectively with positive affirmations. I had used my own affirmations throughout my life and she had often mentioned and repeated the importance of speaking the positive affirmations out loud while looking at your reflection in the mirror.

I encourage you to practice the technique, using affirmations that you can create for yourself regarding the happiness level you want to be in at any moment in time.

There is a powerful sentence I learned in a seminar called "The Basic". The course is a three day seminar, provided by the PSI Seminars Company throughout the United States. In it, I learned a powerful principle stated in a simple yet powerful sentence, "So What? Now What?"

It's true that all of us have gone through hard times and especially painful situations. However, if we keep dwelling on the past and what happened, we will keep being in pain. As I mentioned before, when we live in the past, we bring the old pain into the present and when we worry about what could happen, then we'll feel pain for what does not yet exist and might never come to be. The lesson is to live in the present.

When we say, "So What? Now What?" we have the power to release what happened and **create** a new situation with the experience and the resources we have in this moment. The key here is to **create a life worth living**, a life that is awesome and that fulfills all our needs and desires. A life that will also make a difference in the people around us and those we love. We can even go further and create a life worth living that will be an example to be followed by generations to come.

How would you like to create your life and be someone like Nelson Mandela who lived a life worth living? Or a Mahatma Gandhi, a Mother Theresa, a Louise Hay. Thousands of people have made that difference, and you are no exception. You can also be an example of a life worth living. And guess what? It is all up to you to create that life worth living.

Many people let life happen to them. They enroll in studies or a career they don't like. They take a job that does not satisfy them. They settle for a relationship that happened to them because they got pregnant. Many live a life of resignation because that is not what they originally wanted. And they just accepted what life threw at them. Let me assure you that we all have an option.

We all can start right now, in this moment, to make different choices and create *a life worth living.*

Try this technique: look at yourself in a mirror, and speak out loud what you want to create for your life. Not only for the people around you, for your children and your significant other. See yourself in the mirror exactly the way you want to look in a certain future. See yourself standing tall. See yourself healthy. See yourself full of confidence. See yourself and the people around you precisely the way you want to see them in the future. See your kids graduating from college. See your significant other loving you the way you want love to happen. See it already happening and see yourself in the future completely happy and fulfilled.

The more vivid you see the images in the mirror, the faster they will manifest. In fact, you can see in the mirror the future date in which all be accomplished. See it, listen to the sounds in your head of how it will sound to have that perfect future that makes you happy. Listen to the words your children tell you by appreciating you for what you have done for them. Listen to your significant other telling you how much love she or he feels for you for what you have done for the relationship.

Create that future first in your thoughts and then in front of a mirror and it will happen.

See how your own image changes by saying out loud the affirmations you have created and how, when you see yourself in the future, your smile changes and feels completely different, like you have already accomplished what you declared.

The idea is to practice this technique every morning, when you wake up and are ready to brush your teeth. The perfect moment, since you are already in front of the mirror. You can have your own affirmations written and posted on or near the mirror.

Now, the more vividly you see the images in the mirror of what you want to accomplish, the faster they will become reality. In order to see those images vividly, see your face brilliant and happy, see the color of the things you want to happen sharply, listen to the words you are saying and the words other people speak to you, listen to the sound of your home and possibly the traffic or lack of traffic around your home, listen to the birds and the wind through the tree branches, listen for how it will sound if you were already living **the life worth living** you want to live. See it! Feel it!

Keep practicing until it happens, and then keep creating a better version of your life all the time.

Time is an illusion and will pass faster than you expect of.

Just do it, say it, see it, feel it and make it happen.

Chapter 10

Just "DO IT"

If I can do it, so can you.

In a fabulous speech by **Art Williams**, he says: *"All you can do, is all you can do."*

Why do I mention that speech now? If after all I have said, you just want a simple formula for happiness, here is the formula. Thich Nhat Hanh said, "There Is No Way to Happiness; Happiness Is the Way."

Mr. Art Williams is the one who actually said for the first time, *"DO IT"* now a brand quote used by Nike as *"Just Do It."*

Art figured out that if you want something, you just have to do it, no excuses, nothing. It is a matter of choice and, *"Just Doing It."* Just do what you choose to do.

He tells the story that when he started his life insurance business, for two years he heard the word "NO" over and over and over. However, he kept on *doing* what he believed in, he kept selling life insurance. His reward came after two years when his company paid the beneficiaries of one of the polices he had sold. He tells that without the insurance money, that family would not have been able to pay for the funeral of the deceased. That is when he realized that all those no's he heard and didn't pay attention to them, were the same reason he kept on going and selling, he had a desire to serve other people and he believed in himself, his product and his company. He kept on **DOING IT, AND DOING IT, AND DOING IT.**

When you believe in yourself, you just **DO** what is in your heart and what makes you happy. I encourage you to **JUST DO IT.** *Just do it, just do it, just do it and do it and do it and do it and do it and do it and do it,* until the job gets done.

Art Williams speech from 1987 at the National Religious Broadcaster Convention. Is available on youtube.com at this link:

http://www.youtube.com/watch?v=acXGkGUrf4Q

In that speech, he also says that he encourages everyone on his team, to never say I can't. He actually created a small consequence for anyone who said "I can't" he believes that if you really want something, you'll get it.

So how badly do you want happiness in your life? If you really want happiness, never again say that you can't be happy. Start believing in yourself and believing that you are happy, no matter what is happening in your life, what is happening with the economy, what is happening within your home, or what is happening at your work.

The subject I am writing here about, is the choice of **BEING HAPPY.**

Therefore if you choose to be happy, the only thing you have to do, is *just do it. Be Happy.* No matter what is going on in your life. *Just do it, and do it, and do it, and do it, and do it, and do it, and do it, and do it, and be happy.*

Talking about disposition:

Here is a word worth analyzing, **DISPOSITION!**

What does it mean to you?

What do you understand when the word is used in a sentence?

What disposition do you need in order to be happy?

A friend of mine. Frank Iñiguez wrote a book called: What are you looking for?

Actually, it is called: Que Buscas? The book is in Spanish and in this book, **Frank Iñiguez** says: *"Disposition is the miracle that causes Creation."* When I read this statement, I realized how true it is. If you really have the disposition to be happy, you will create happiness in your life.

Happiness is a state of disposition regarding happiness. If you really, really, really want to be happy, you **must** have a **huge disposition** to **BE HAPPY**, and then you easily will achieve that state of happiness you desire in your life.

All it takes is choice and disposition and working consciously every moment to keep your ego quiet and choose happiness. The ego will want to get you out of your happiness and start making mayhem for everything and everyone. You can choose who will control the moment, your ego or your higher self.

Wikipedia, defines disposition as follows:

> *"Disposition is a habit, a preparation, a state of readiness, or a tendency to act in a specified way."*

Every accomplishment in life has a degree of *disposition* in it. Everything accomplished through time has this important concept attached to it. *Disposition*, if you just get a glimpse of the importance of this concept of *disposition* and you start making of it a habit, your whole life will have a profound change. *Disposition* will make you accomplish any goal you set up to get. I know that when you have the proper *disposition*, you will achieve anything you desire. In this book, I am talking about the choice of happiness. If you apply the concept of *disposition* to achieve the happiness that you want, I am certain that you will have that desired happiness.

I invite you to have the habit or *disposition* of being happy all the time.

Every morning when you wake up, just say to yourself: **"YES I CAN, IT IS EASY AND I AM HAPPY,"** no matter what.

Chapter 11

Easy to do, easy not to do.

This chapter is the shortest, because it goes straight to the point. And if followed, will achieve the happiness everyone seeks, simply and easily.

It was originally going to be Chapter 4. However, it is the last chapter I am writing and therefore I am relocating the chapter to the end, just before the chapter of: "A year of happiness through affirmations."

> *"The First duty of all human beings is to be Happy...*
> *Second, is to make other people happy"*
>
> *-Mario Moreno "Cantinflas"-*

The title of the chapter is **Easy to do, Easy not to do.** I learned this concept from one of the greatest books I have ever read. <u>The Slight Edge</u> by Jeff Olson. He explains the concept **(Easy to do, easy not to do)** in detail and says that most of the things that create happiness in our lives, like health, wealth and all other great and good things that we desire out of life, are really easy to do, and easy not to do. Thinking of the valuable concept of these words, I named this chapter after Jeff Olson's concept of Easy to do, Easy not to do, because achieving happiness is just like that, easy. Easy to be happy or easy not to be happy. It is your choice that will make it so. Jeff Olson explores deeper into the concept. He applies the compound interest concept to the idea of, "Easy to do or Easy not to do". So, anything you do or don't do will increase in a surprising way after some time. If happiness is what we are talking about, then after a few days, months and years, you will be either the happiest person on Earth or the most miserable and it will only have to do with your choice of being happy each moment of your life as a matter of choice.

Easy to do, Easy not to do. The choice is yours and I suggest you read Jeff Olson's book, The Slight Edge. The concept: Easy to do or Easy not to do, is thoroughly explained.

What you have to do is just **"Do It."** Be Happy; Hakuna Matata, which is a Swahili phrase that means 'no worries'. If you saw the movie Lion King by Disney Studios, which was their 32nd animated feature. There is a song, sung by three characters; Timon (a meerkat), Pumbaa (a warthog), and Simba, a young lion. The musical was written by Elton John and the lyrics by Tim Rice. And the point of the song is to be happy no matter what, have no worries, live in the now and enjoy it. ***JUST DO IT.***

There is another book written by Dr. Wayne Dyer, titled: Gifts from Eykis he mentioned once that the original title was going to be: If You Want to Be Happy, Get Your Head Out Of Uranus. Since it included more serious content, he ended naming the book: Gifts From Eykis. I highly suggest its reading. There is a link below of a short talk by Dr. Wayne Dyer about his book in the following YouTube page:

https://www.youtube.com/watch?v=j36m6JfywPg

In his book; Dyer makes a parody about people having anxiety attacks and how an alien from Uranus, when visiting the Earth, finds out that even though both planets are almost the same, in Uranus, anxiety really attacks not like in Earth where anxiety is just a perception of our ego.

Anxiety, fear, worries, preoccupation and all other false perceptions that seem real, are only creations of our ego. It is something that can disappear like Dr. Wayne Dyer says, just by snapping our fingers and deciding to *"Just Do It"*. So, I invite you to *"JUST DO IT."*

Be happy, *Just do it.* Be as happy as you want to be, *Just Do it, Just Do It and JUST DO IT.* I will repeat like Art Williams, *Just Do It, and keep on doing it, and doing it, and doing it, and doing it, and doing it, and doing it.*

If at any time you think you can't, just watch the YouTube videos I suggested and bring that state of happiness with a snap of your fingers, *just do it.*

My last youtube.com suggestion is a visit to a shrink, the best shrink doctor you have ever seen or have ever existed. (Of course it's a parody).

He just heals people in one, yes only one visit to his office. He is the greatest Psychology practitioner that I have ever seen in action. I highly recommend you to follow his advice and if you do, it will help you to be happy at any time. You can see his method on youtube.com. You'll be glad and you will be cured from worries, fear and anxiety very easily.

Here is a link for the video in youtube.com:
https://www.youtube.com/watch?v=EAlWBhohDp4

End of the chapter and end of the book.

JUST DO IT, BE HAPPY, IT'S REALLY EASY TO DO

Now follow, "A Year of Happiness Through Affirmations". In the last chapter, my best wishes to you and happy life forever. My love and my heart full of happiness goes to all of you who read this book.

Appendix

A Year of Happiness through affirmations

Next concept: HAPPY 365 Affirmations for the day, creating a new program in your subconscious mind, the HAPPY program. Fake it until you make it.

This is a way to program my mind with a happy attitude. After 30 days of repeating happy thoughts, my subconscious mind will be programmed with happiness; it will be easier to choose happiness.

1.- I choose to be happy today. If the concept is too hard for you to accept, modify it to I choose to be happy for the next minute, then the next 5 minutes, and keep raising the number of minutes until you can believe you can be happy for an hour, eventually your small successes will create a program in your subconscious mind that will help you to believe that you are successful at anything if you can break it down to small goals.

2.- I live in the now and right now I choose to feel happy.

3.- My happiness comes from within.

4.- It's not what is happening around me what makes me happy is how I interpret what happens now.

5.- I believe I can choose to be happy at any moment.

6.- My beliefs make me happy.

7.- All that happens today makes me feel happy.

8.- I am inoculated with the virus of happiness, HDAV; a great meme to have in my mind.

9.- I focus on happiness and happiness shows in my life because I attract happiness.

10.- The only feeling in me is happiness, it is my natural way of being, the way I was created by infinite intelligence.

11.- Paradise is here and NOW, and paradise was originally created for me to be happy.

12.- By sharing my happiness I create a world of happy people around me.

13.- The word happiness, sounds like divine music into my ears.

14.- I am aware of my choices to be happy.

15.- Yeah, I am happy now.

16.- Today my feelings are happy feelings.

17.- I create a happy day today.

18.- I love my happy life.

19.- I am responsible for feeling happy.

20.- My choices today will create a happy feeling all day.

21.- I am a successful choosing happiness today.

22.- It is easy for me to be happy.

23.- Today my choices create happy moments all day.

24.- I am responsible of my happy thoughts and my happy choices.

25.- My nick name is "HAPPY".

26.- I see happy people around me all the time.

27.- Happy thoughts come to my mind easily.

28.- I create happy moments all day.

29.- I am in charge of my happy thoughts.

30.- I attract happy people.

31.- Happiness surrounds me all the time.

32.- I live in a happy place.
33.- Whatever happens today around me has nothing to do with my happy feelings.
34.- I radiate happiness and the people I meet today see it and want part of the happiness I radiate.
35.- I increase my happiness day by day.
36.- Happy thoughts come easy today.
37.- A smile in my face, doesn't mean absence of problems, but the ability to be happy, above all problems.
38.- I am happy because I can.
39.- I am happy NOW and always.
40.- I am happy no matter what.
41.- Today and every day I become happier and happier.
42.- Happiness is a blessing at all times.
43.- I am happy and I feel happy at any moment I choose to.
44.- I am aware of my happiness and my feelings all the time.
45.- Feeling happy is awesome and I am feeling happy NOW.
46.- The happy effect lives in me.
47.- I am the personification of happiness.
48.- I am happy, happy, happy all day long.
49.- I love being happy.
50.- My happiness makes my day AWESOME and my life worth living.
51.- It is very easy to be happy all the time.
52.- Today is my day of full happiness.
53.- Now I realize how easy is to be happy all the time.
54.- I love being happy again, again and again.
55.- I know I am a being made of love and happiness.
56.- I was created to be happy therefore I am happy now.
57.- I am created by love and love is happiness, so I am the personification of happiness now.
58.- Today, you are you, you are love and you are happy.

59.- Today is a happier day than yesterday.

60.- Today I enjoy the feeling of being happy.

61.- Every day and everywhere I go I am happier and happier.

62.- Today all people I find and greet, is people I make happy with my smile.

63.- Finding happiness is very easy, I find happy people all the time and I enjoy it.

64.- My happiness comes from within me.

65.- I radiate happiness and other people notice and they become happier.

66.- My happiness is contagious, and I help make people happy.

67.- What I give I receive, therefore I am giving happiness with my smiles and my attitude.

68.- I am the personification of happiness.

69.- The energy of God dwells in me and this energy is pure happiness.

70.- I embrace the quality of God that is Love, and that makes me Happy.

71.- Being happy is easier than being in some other state.

72.- The more happy, the more I enjoy life.

73.- Happiness is a choice and it is an easy choice.

74.- My imperfections make me happy.

75.- The more I know me, the more happy I become.

76.- The more I give of me, the more happy I am.

77.- When I am with others, it is easier and easier to be happy.

78.- When I help others I feel happier and happier, therefore I like to help others.

79.- When I change my attitude, my happiness increases.

80.- Every day it is easier and easier to make other people happy and that increases my happiness too.

81.- I just found that giving of me, makes me happier.

82.- A smile in my face makes people happy and I make myself happier.

83.- When I help others I feel happy. I want to help many people.

84.- Giving is receiving and that makes me happy.

85.- As I learn to be happy, more people around me are happier.

86.- The simple life makes me happy.

87.- Trees, flowers and nature make me happy.

88.- City, pavement and buildings make me happy.

89.- When I see a vegetable sprout, I see life and joy and happiness inundate my being.

90.- Love all, and love everything, and when I do, happiness comes to me.

91.- I am surrounded by happy thoughts.

92.- Happy is my name.

93.- I am loving being happy all the time.

94.- How easy is to be happy.

95.- Happiness pours out of every porous of my skin.

96.- God made me happy, when I choose not to feel happy, I am choosing not to listen to God.

97.- Circumstances do not dictate my happiness, I do.

98.- My past experience of sadness, do not determines my future joy and happiness.

99.- Life is like a Rubik's cube it seems all scrambled and my happiness lies in putting each side, of one color, and when I do, I start all over again.

100.- I am happy because today, I have one hundred affirmations of happiness I can practice with.

101.- I look forward for another one hundred happiness affirmations in the next one hundred days, Yes that makes me happy.

102.- Now I understand that being happy is completely my choice.

103.- Every day my choices of being happy are easier and easier.

104.- Easy comes, and easy stays, being happy is very Easy.

105.- I am embracing happiness all the time.

106.- My state of happiness is my consciousness of constant Joy.

107.- I am the personification of love, Joy and happiness.

108.- The happier I am, the happier other people become around me.

109.- I am contributing to the 100 monkey effect of happiness in the world with my choice of happiness.

110.- I see happy people all around me even if they do not know they are happy, and that makes me happy.

111.- Today is the 111 happy number, I search and find three happy people that will make 111 people happy.

112.- I speak happiness to people and I convince them that they are happy all the time by choice.

113.- When I contribute to make more people happy, I become happier.

114.- It is very easy to make people to be happy.

115.- More and more people see me happy and they become happy, I am a contagious happiness.

116.- Simple things make me happy all the time.

117.- I feel the happiness surging through my being.

118.- If I was created to the Image and likeness of God and God is Happy, then I am happy.

119.- Happiness is my natural state of being.

120.- I feel Joy and I exude Joy and people around me become happy and joyful.

121.- My happiness is contagious, therefore I am responsible of being happy so others can be happy.

122.- I realize that happiness comes from within.

123.- The feeling of love brings happiness to me, I choose to be loving to everything so I can feel happy.

124.- I remember happy moments of my past and that makes me happy.

125.- I can choose to feel sad or happy and being happy is a lot better, so I choose to feel happy.

126.- I share my happiness with everyone I meet today, so I am aware to be happy all the time.

127.- Relentless happiness surrounds me all the time.

128.- Life is an expression of joy and happiness, just look around and see happy events.

129.- Wherever I turn, I see happy people and happy animals and happy events.

130.- If in one side of my life there is something I don't like I turn to the other side where happiness is waiting for me.

131.- The more I see happiness, the more I find happiness.

132.- Happy people are attracted to me and I give happiness to all.

133.- What I give I receive, so I choose to give my best happy face today.

134.- For me to be happy is easy, I just remember when I was happy in my past.

135.- I send happy thoughts to my future, so when I get there I will be happy.

136.- Remembering the happiness of my past, makes me happy today and in the future.

137.- When I am happy, I generate endorphins in my body and the effect makes me more happy.

138.- Love, Joy and happiness are within me all the time, I see it and I feel it.

139.- Happiness is a feeling that I can generate from within any time I choose to.

140.- There is no better choice to be happy all the time.

141.- I plant in my brain the idea of being happy always.

142.- I have mastered being happy by choice.

143.- I am conscious and aware of me being happy by choice.

144.- I am willing to be my best at being happy today.

145.- Today the desire I fulfill is to be happy.

146.- I just realize that I can be happy without drinking any kind of alcohol.

147.- Everything I do, brings me happiness today.

148.- I choose to work on something that makes me happy today.

149.- If I make other people happy, I feel happy myself.

150.- I see happiness all around me, from the flower I found while walking and by meeting people today.

151.- Children are happy with anything new, I choose to see new things today that make me happy.

152.- When I become like a child, I am happy all the time, so I choose to be like a child.

153.- Thinking of someone I love, makes me happy, I choose to think of people I love.

154.- I see joy and happiness around me all the time, I identify myself with happiness.

155.- Words can bring happiness, I choose the words that make me happy.

156.- Trusting others makes me happy, I trust life and all people around me.

157.- I breath happiness and happiness breaths me, happiness and me are one.

158.- I speak happiness to all, and happiness is spoken to me from within.

159.- My heavenly knowledge is pure happiness.

160.- The purpose of my creation was to be happy, therefore I embrace the happiness I was created for.

161.- I vibrate happiness, and I manifest happiness.

162.- I, in my desire to serve others, give happiness to everyone I meet.

163.- Me alone, I'm responsible for my happiness and the happiness of the people around me.

164.- My word speaks happiness, and hearing it creates happiness in others.

165.- My power lies in being happy, I am powerful because I am very happy.

166.- Happiness is like a fruit, it ripens with my happy thoughts.

167.- When I feel ONE with God I feel happy.

168.- Happiness can be achieved by pulling the layers of the onion of sadness and grief My Onion center turns to sweet happiness.

169.- I can wait to be happy some day, however I rather be happy NOW.

170.- I give a message of joy and happiness to everyone I meet today and that makes me happy.

171.- There is no explanation of my happiness, I am just happy for no reason.

172.- The meaning of life is to be happy, so what am I waiting for? I am happy now.

173.- There is nothing to explain or comprehend to be happy, just be happy.

174.- The best way to live, is being happy, so be happy for no reason.

175.- When I am happy, I exude happiness, and everyone feels it and loves it.

176.- Happiness is the natural state of life, I am in paradise, which means to be happy all the time, I choose to see paradise expressing around me all the time.

177.- Choice is all there is. Choose happiness.

178.- Today I am so happy and is so easy to be happy.

179.- My happiness is my credo, and my motto, I spread happiness around me.

180.- Thank you God for letting me be an expression of happiness for all human kind.

181.- When I feel happy, I am like a generator of Universal happiness for the whole Universe.

182.- My happiness makes other people happy, and I want to make other people happy all the time.

183.- Being thankful makes me happy, I am thankful for my life, my friends, my parents, my children and my partner.

184.- I realize that living in the past or the future, makes me anxious, therefore I live in the now where I can be happy.

185.- When I choose to love my life, being happy is easy.

186.- If I do not love what I do for a living, I can choose to change that and make a life worth living that will make me happy.

187.- Outside stuff doesn't make me happy, I realize that happiness comes from within.

188.- When I see things in a different way, things itself change, so I have the power to change everything I see, to happy things and happy endings.

189.- My beliefs create my surroundings, my beliefs are of happy thoughts that create happy moments.

190.- It is so easy to be happy, so I choose happy beingness.

191.- My choices, bring the same choices in other people, so I choose to be happy so more people are happy with me.

192.- It is so easy to be happy, it is just a choice, and an easy one.

193.- The quality of my choices determine the quality of my future, I choose happy thoughts so I can have a happy future.

194.- Happiness and Joy is a vibration of the Spirit, my Spirit is God's Spirit and it's vibration is Joy and happiness, therefore I am happiness and Joy.

195.- The mystery of happiness is within me, I discover how easy is to be happy.

196.- My Spiritual personality expresses happiness all the time.

197.- The I AM within me is the I AM that spoke to Abraham by the burning bushes, and that I AM is pure happiness, which is Me expressing itself through Me as happiness.

198.- I have dream happiness and now I make my happiness dreams come true.

199.- Life was meant to be lived in Joy and happiness, I obey the law of happiness by being happy now.

200.- I can think happy thoughts now and all the time.

201.- My life is full of Joy and happiness all the time.

202.- The vibration of happiness is the vibration that I like and I tune my body on the vibration of joy and happiness now, because my body is like a radio tuning to happiness now.

203.- My heart radiates happiness for all and receives happiness from all.

204.- The center of my being is happy, and my center is the Center of a Happy Universe.

205.- There is no good or bad, those are only labels we put on things, when I realize that, Happiness is the center of all.

206.- My happiness do not depend on others or external things, happiness is my state of beingness.

207.- When I am separate of my higher self, I separate myself from happiness, so I choose to go back to my higher self and return to happiness.

208.- Who am I is Happiness, Joy and Love.

209.- I love being happy and it is addictive.

210.- My core being is happiness, what a Joy.

211.- My happiness comes from within my higher self which is God itself.

212.- When I realize who am I, it is so easy to be happy and creative like the Universe.

213.- There is only one way of being and that way is to be happy, else only excuses.

214.- My happiness is God's happiness.

215.- I am thriving in Happiness and Joy now and all the time.

216.- My happiness fuels the Universe with more happiness, I am a generator of Happiness for the Universe.

217.- I am conscious of my role in the Universe, therefore, I fulfill it by being happy all the time, that generates the energy of Joy and happiness for all the Universe, I am one with the Universe.

218.- Loving thoughts, bring Joy and happiness to my mind.

219.- My reaction to the events in my life, are the results of the programs in my human mind, If I understand that, I can change my reaction to a love reaction, it will bring happiness to my life.

220.- I choose to change the programs that make me feel unhappy for new ways of thinking that bring Joy and happiness to my life every day.

221.- My life is directed by Joy and happiness, I choose to be that way.

222.- When my mind is full of happy thoughts, there is no space for any other kind of thought.

223.- I am feeling Joy and happiness now and all the time by choice.

224.- I am the source, I am the one that chooses, I am choosing happiness always, I am happiness embodied.

225.- My being is happiness, my body is happy, my mind is happy, I am Happy.

226.- Going through life could be challenging, Happiness is challenging and I beat challenges by being happy.

227.- I now realize that it is very easy to be happy, it is just a choice.

228.- I command happiness in my life all the time.

229.- I am the creator and the generator of Joy and happiness and I do create happiness and Joy in my life.

230.- I scream and shout loud, and that creates endorphins that make me happy.

231.- My life is awesome and it is better than many other people around the world and that makes me happy and thankful.

232.- I am happy because I am thankful.

233.- My thoughts, determine my feelings, if I control my thoughts, I can control my feelings and I choose to think to be happy.

234.- When I see myself in the mirror, I can see I am not what I think of me, so if I am not what I think of me, what am I? I am that I AM. and I am all there is. I AM HAPPY, I am the creator of my life.

235.- Ego is the cause of unhappiness, I choose to edge ego out and bring my higher self in to being happy.

236.- I was meant to be happy, therefore I AM.

237.- My nature is happiness, I honor my nature by being happy all the time.

238.- I enjoy happiness, why would I choose to be out of it?

239.- Happiness is my nature, I honor my nature and spread my nature to others to awaken them to happiness.

240.- My joy is your Joy, my happiness is your happiness, I am responsible for your happiness. I am happy so you can be happy.

241.- My happiness brings you happiness and everybody into happiness.

242.- I am responsible for the happiness of the world, so I choose happiness all the time to spread infinite happiness around the world.

243.- My happiness is your happiness.

244.- I so much enjoy your happiness that I am happy for you and that makes and creates happiness for others.

245.- Sending happiness to others makes me happy, and makes the energy of happiness circulate without limits.

246.- My thoughts of Joy and Happiness are the generators and dynamos of more Joy and Happiness in others.

247.- Being happy, is just an idea. I think happy thoughts and then prove the results for myself.

248.- I have love within myself and loving thoughts make me happy.

249.- Love is a Universal energy, I am made of Love, love between my parents and Love from the Universe. Love is joy and happiness, therefore I am Joy and happiness.

250.- All people I meet today, smile at me and are nice with me, that makes me happy.

251.- I am conscious of my choices today and my choices are happy choices.

252.- Today I give smiles and love to each person I speak to, and I receive double energy of love, joy and happiness.

253.- I am happy and I am contagious.

254.- I speak kind words to people all the time and that makes a difference in the attitude of the people I meet, I am living a life worth living just because of my kind words that make people happy.

255.- By me being happy, I am contributing to a happy world, helping to create a critical mass of consciousness of joy and happiness.

256.- I make a difference in the joy and happiness of others, because I am happy.

257.- It is very easy to be happy, I just think happy thoughts and smile.

258.- I choose to create a positive view of any event that happens in my life and that makes me happy.

259.- I feel happy when I remember my loved ones, this thoughts are send to my loved ones and they feel happy.

260.- I am aware that I am alive today and that makes me happy.

261.- I am breathing and I feel the life in my veins and blood, I am thankful for my life and that makes me happy.

262.- I surrender to the Happiness feeling, I embrace Happiness in love.

263.- My words and my affirmations create happiness around me all the time.

264.- I am Conscious of bringing happiness to my everyday life.

265.- My eyes see happiness all the time, therefore I feel happy all day.

266.- I am enamored with the possibility of being happy now.

267.- Me and my happiness are one, I feel happy and I Am happy.

268.- I believe that I am happy now.

269.- Every cell of my body is happy and healthy, therefore I am happy and healthy.

270.- I am perfect just the way I AM, and that makes me happy, my imperfection is perfect in the realm of the Universe.

271.- I AM happy because I realize that I have all the qualities of the Creator, I am love, I am creative, I am energy, I am light, I am generous.

272.- I am a giver and that makes me happy, I give love, I give my time, I give my presence, I give myself just the way I am.

273.- I desire to be happy, and therefore I create ideas that make me happy now.

274.- I receive smiles and kindness from all people I found in my path and that makes me happy.

275.- I am capable to help make a better world and that makes me happy.

276.- I can create a future full of happiness all the time.

277.- I am happy now, because what has happened before has no power on my present.

278.- My ultimate freedom is my ability to create by choice my happiness.

279.- Just today I am happy, and I repeat these words every day of my life.

280.- I realize that there is always a place in me that is always happy.

281.- My true value, lies in my capability of choosing happiness over anything else.

282.- I am helping someone today and that will make me happy.

283.- Each tiny effort to be happy, builds on the next one, so little by little I am happier and happier.

284.- I believe in myself and my capability of being happy now.

285.- My life is to be enjoyed and my purpose today is to be happy.

286.- If I have been a caterpillar hiding in a cocoon, Now I break my prison and spread my butterfly wings in joy and happiness.

287.- I am alive to count my blessings and that makes me happy.

288.- I am in a state of happiness by realizing I am already there.

289.- I am so happy like if today were my last day.

290.- My thoughts create my happiness moment by moment.

291.- One choice and one choice, one by one, I am choosing day by day happiness in my life.

292.- If I can share my happiness with one person each day, I am helping to create a better world.

293.- I am moving forward with happiness instead of being stop by my problems.

294.- I enjoy freedom and freedom makes me happy.

295.- I maintain healthy relationships and instead of making others happy, I create happiness for myself, and the fact I am happy, makes the others happy because I am happily contagious.

296.- I see wonderful things around me all the time and I give thanks for my capability of seen them as wonderful and beautiful, the feeling is joy and happiness.

297.- I am responsible for the way I feel and I choose to feel happy now.

298.- I am an expression of God's creation and as such I am perfect and I am happy.

299.- I am a personalized expression of divinity, just thinking about it, makes me happy.

300.- I choose to live and feel the now, and now I am happy, I do not live in the past neither in the future and my now is perfectly happy.

301.- Just the thought of the possibility of being happy, makes me happy now, I create my own happiness by thinking happy thoughts.

302.- I create a new purpose for my life and this new purpose is to be happy every day.

303.- I feel whole when I am happy and since happiness is a choice I choose to be happy now.

304.- My happiness is in my mind and I command my mind to be happy now.

305.- I shift my consciousness to happiness, I create happiness just by pure desire to be happy.

306.- I AM that I AM, and that I am is eternal and the thought of being eternal and whole makes me happy, knowing that nothing can harm me and I am and always will be.

307.- I Am the thinker behind my thoughts and the Thinker is eternally happy, I Am happy.

308.- I dream awake of happy thoughts and I create a realm of happiness now.

309.- I can create ecstasy within, to think is to create and I create happiness always.

310.- I am Spirit and I am inspired to create happiness, I inspire myself and others to be happy now.

311.- Life reveals happiness all the time around me, I keep on seeing happy people and happy animals and happy plants, my whole world is happy.

312.- My outer expression is full of joy and happiness and I attract happy people and happy events to my life.

313.- Everything I experience I can Interpret as I desire, I can choose to experience happiness, which is better than anything else.

314.- I choose to turn away anything that doesn't make me happy.

315.- Happiness comes naturally and easy to me.

316.- When I choose Love over anything else, I feel Happy.

317.- I choose compassion instead of anger, I choose happiness instead of suffering.

318.- My discipline pays me with the capability of choosing how I feel, everyday is easier and easier to be happy.

319.- I plant happy thoughts in my brain and these happy thoughts grow like beautiful trees of joy.

320.- I Know that my subconscious mind, manages all my body functions like the circulatory system and digestive system, now I give orders to my subconscious mind to manage my state of joy and happiness to the fullest and perfect bliss.

321.- Happiness is a Divine Idea and I make it mine so I am happy all the time.

322.- I was born and meant to be happy, my only purpose in life is to make other people happy and that in turn makes me happy.

323.- I am a Master Teacher of Joy and Happiness, in order to teach I learn first to be happy.

324.- My body claims happiness, my body enjoys happiness, I give nourishment and happiness to my body.

325.- I LOVE TO BE HAPPY.

326.- I think happiness and my thoughts become reality.

327.- I promise myself each morning to be happy, no matter what happens during the day.

328.- When I think happy thoughts, I attract happy moments.

329.- I am an embodiment of the energy of Joy and happiness.

330.- Each cell of my body works better when I am happy, I send happy thoughts to all the cells of my body.

331.- The energy that my whole body emanates is pure joy and happiness, I emanate Joy and happiness.

332.- I am a generator of Happiness and all people around me feel it.

333.- Today I send happiness to all people around me and they reflect that happiness to all people they meet today.

334.- Happiness is reproducing itself all the time around me and people respond according to the feelings I send to them.

335.- I am more loving and happy each day with everyone I meet.

336.- I create happiness from within and I give my happiness to all, the more I give happiness, the more happy I am.

337.- My life is easier and smoother when I am happy, then I choose to be happy all the time.

338.- I used to dream to be happy, now I am a happy dreamer.

339.- I store happiness in each cell of my body and I am full of happy thoughts exuding happiness all the time.

340.- My name is Joy, my last name is Happy .

341.- Now I am used to being happy I wear clothes of happiness and Joy all the time.

342.- By now I am so strong in my belief of joy and happiness that people feel it and they become happy in my presence.

343.- My behavior and my actions speak louder than my words and I radiate happiness without speaking it.

344.- Happiness is the bread and wine of life, I survive with the energy of happiness.

345.- I speak, feel and radiate happiness wherever I go.

346.- My life is full of joy, love and happiness now.

347.- My thoughts create my reality, therefore I choose to think happy thoughts.

348.- I am the Master of my life, the commander of my thoughts and my behavior, I command happiness as my beingness now.

349.- My results are based on my thoughts and actions, I produce happy results based on my thoughts and actions.

350.- I know I can control my thoughts and my feelings, and I choose to feel happy and think happy thoughts.

351.- I am surrounded by happy people, I am happy with them.

352.- I remember happy moments all the time, It is my choice what do I want to remember.

353.- I trust life and life brings happiness all the time to me.

354.- I create happy thoughts very easy, is easy for me to be happy all the time by focusing happy thoughts and seeing happiness all around me.

355.- By being happy I make other people happy and that makes more happiness in my world.

356.- Every day is easier and easier to be happy.

357.- Now I know that I am the creator of the way my life is, and I choose to create happy moments now and always.

358.- I attract happiness and happy people to my life every day.

359.- Christmas memories bring happiness to my heart, I bring Christmas memories now and I am happy.

360.- Material gifts also bring happiness to my life.

361.- Loving people surround me all the time and that makes me happy.

362.- Knowing that everything has a start and an end, makes me understand that everything must past and I accept that with Joy and happiness, endings are also beginnings.

363.- My heart is full of gratitude and that makes me happy.

364.- Ends do not mean sorrow, end means change for the better, and that makes me happy.

365.- MY ONLY PURPOSE IN LIFE IS TO BE HAPPY. I KNOW I AM HAPPY NOW.

Conclusion

As you can see, having a happy and joyous lifestyle has tremendous benefits. But happiness doesn't just happen, it is a matter of choice. In the beginning, it will be an effort to keep your focus on being happy. Soon, that effort will become a habit and the constant choice will be effortless. Then, you will have achieved constant and effective happiness that will bring to your life many benefits in health and joy, as well as new and better relationships and abundance that will come to you without any additional effort. You have to choose your thoughts, just as a gardener chooses the seeds for his garden. Then water your happy seeds with gratitude, laughter and appreciation for all that is happening in your life.

> *"A Man asked Lord Buddha, 'I WANT HAPPINESS'*
> *Lord Buddha said:*
> *'First remove "I". That's ego.*
> *Then remove "Want". That's desire.'*
> *See, now you are left with only HAPPINESS"*
>
> *-Unknown-*

About the Author

Rico Ituarte.

Federico "Rico" Ituarte was born in 1948 in Mexico City, the second son of a middle class couple. His father was a truncated lawyer who aspired to be an artist with great capability in drawing and modern abstract art. His mother who took care of the three children and was an entrepreneur, sold everything that came into her hands and created a new business that serviced several Government agencies. Federico as the middle child, mediated all conflicts between peers and family. He studied business administration and worked as manager for his mother's business until he married and moved to California to have his first Daughter and later his son. He then moved back to Mexico to the beautiful port of Acapulco, where he succeeded as a director of several companies.

He later divorced and moved back to California, participated in a Church as a member of the board of directors and studied most of world religions. After that, he started his quest for happiness creating a life of liberty and joy, and helps the Latino community by participating as facilitator in self improving seminars. His passion is to help people be all they can be.

Sources

- Ackerman, Kenneth J, Ph.D. "The Universal People." (May 13, 2009) http://www.udel.edu/anthro/ackerman/universal_people.pdf
- Data Face. "Facial Expression: A Primary Communication System." (May 14, 2009)http://www.face-and-emotion.com/dataface/expression/expression.jsp
- Devlin, Kate. "Missing facial muscles make some look glum." The Daily Telegraph. June 17, 2008. http://www.telegraph.co.uk/scienceandtechnology/science/sciencenews/3344681/Missing-facial-muscles-make-some-look-glum.html
- Ekman, Paul; et al. "Final Report To NSF of the Planning Workshop on Facial Expression Understanding." Aug. 1, 1992.http://www.face-and-emotion.com/dataface/nsfrept/nsf_contents.html
- Foreman, Judy. "A Conversation with: Paul Ekman; The 43 Facial Muscles That Reveal Even the Most Fleeting Emotions." The New York Times. Aug. 5, 2003. http://www.nytimes.com/2003/08/05/health/conversation-with-paul-ekman-43-facial-muscles-that-reveal-even-most-fleeting.html
- Lewis, Michael. Handbook of emotions (second edition). Guilford Press, 2004. ISBN 1593850298, 9781593850296.http://books.google.com/books?id=SQ8F7zdhORwC&printsec=frontcover#PPA236,M1
- Nicolay, Christopher W., Ph.D. Associate Professor, UNCA Department of Biology. E-mail correspondence. May 14, 2009.
- Patel, Alpen A., MD. "Facial Nerve Anatomy." Mar. 18, 2009. http://emedicine.medscape.com/article/835286-overview)

Printed in the United States
By Bookmasters